Jenuine Poetry for Life

POEMS TO UPLIFT HUMANITY

Jen Ward

Jenuine Healing
Wodonga, Australia

Copyright © 2022 by Jen Ward.

This work is subject to copyright. All rights are reserved. No part of this publication may be reproduced, distributed, or transmitted in any form or by any means, including photocopying, recording, or other electronic or mechanical methods, without the prior written permission of the publisher, except in the case of brief quotations embodied in critical reviews and certain other noncommercial uses permitted by copyright law. For permission requests, write to the publisher, addressed 'Attention: Permissions Coordinator,' at the address below.

Jen Ward / Jenuine Healing
https://www.jenuinehealing.com/contact-jen

Jenuine Poetry for Life/ Jen Ward.

ISBN 978-1-7351056-3-5

Table of Contents

Foreword xi
Jenuine Healing on Social Media xxvii

Universal Consciousness 1
   May All Blessings Be 7
   The Fight 9
   The Apathy of Man 10
   Pure Love 12
   A State of Being 13
   Perceiving in Energy 14
   Individuality 16
   Balance 17
   Being Present 18
   Love in the End 19
   A Portal of God 21
   All Life 22
   Human Victory 23

The Human Collective 25
   The Gift of This Life's Struggle 31
   Second Sight 34
   Shadows Come Alive 35
   Humanity 36
   I Am Love 38
   A Distant God 39
   Life's Monument 41
   Buying Freedom 43
   The Example 44
   What Needs to Happen to Have Peace 47
   Love's Beautiful Array 49

Getting to the Heart of It *51*
Give a Life Its Due *53*
Bonded in Purpose *55*
Silent Majority *57*
Love's Best Lesson *59*
Your Average Best Friend *60*
Speaking for the Unborn *61*
The Tiny Fleet of Sandy Hook Angels *62*
The Sledgehammer *64*
Beautiful Androgyny *66*
To Finally Expound *67*

Nature 69
Homage to the Foliage *76*
Sighting *78*
Mortar and Sticks *79*
GMOs *80*
H$_2$0 .... *82*
More than Family *83*
Any Day *84*
The Moment *85*
Gaia Speaks *86*
One and the Same *88*

Ascension 89
Winning the Human Race *99*
Transcendence *101*
Every Angel *103*
Awakening *104*
The Awakened *105*
Artistry *106*
Living in Zen *107*
Soul Trail Blazer *108*
Incarnating *109*
That's What You Do *110*

Omniscience *113*
A New Person *114*
Self-Realization *116*
Mastery *117*
What It Is to Be Free *118*
Enlightenment *119*
How to Transcend *120*
Encouragement of a Full Moon *121*
Your Friend *122*

Self-Awareness 123
   Men of Goddess *127*
   Monastery *129*
   The Empath *130*
   I'm Me *131*
   A Series of Blessings *132*
   Gaining Spiritual Maturity *134*
   Love's Own Decree *136*
   The Golden Thing *140*
   Thrill Ride *141*
   Goddesses' Plea *142*
   How? *143*
   Empowerment *144*
   Between the Stillness and the Sky *145*
   All This and More *147*

Soul Mate 149
   The Betterment of You *154*
   My Altar *155*
   The Valley Past Time *156*
   Your Happiness *158*
   To Empower the World *159*
   Healing All Souls *160*
   I Honor You *162*
   You Are the Victor *164*

One Worthy Goal...... *165*
Qualities *166*
God or Source *167*
Spiritual Marriage...... *168*
One Loving Plea *169*
Surrender...... *170*
Senses *171*
The Ultimate Goal *172*
My Alchemy *173*

Healing Goddess 175
Healers Reunite *179*
Wounded Goddess *181*
Loving by Default *182*
Commitment to Me *183*
Meet Me Halfway *185*
Permission...... *187*
Assistance *188*
Humanity's Greatest Vice *189*
Proving Me Wrong *191*
Through Your Eyes...... *192*
The Replanting *194*
The Winter Rose *195*
The Defense *196*
Guiding Light Source *198*
When Childhood Goes Wrong...... *200*

Living a Spiritual Life...... 201
Angel's Hue *208*
Turning Point *210*
The Wayshower *212*
Love Is All You Are...... *214*
When?...... *216*
Truth *217*
Within You...... *218*

- Love's Compassion 219
- Where Truth and Love Began 220
- The Celebration 221
- An Easy Sell 223
- You Exponentially 225
- Book of Life 227
- Sing 228
- Discernment 229
- Love's Appeal 230
- We Can 232
- Celebrating the Moment of Now 234
- Integrity's Blueprint 235
- Love's Final Decree 236
- Bless This Day 238
- Integrity's By-Laws 239
- The Depth of You 240

Inspiration 241
- Encouragement 244
- What Would Dr. Seuss Say? 245
- One Little Human 248
- One Little Human: The Dichotomy 249
- Yet 250
- Homage to You 251
- Loved on All Sides 252
- The Miracle of You 253
- What You Are Capable Of 254
- Beauty 255
- Live Life Boldly! 256
- True Abundance 257
- True Strength 258
- One Ancient Celestial Tune 260
- The Troubadour 262

Searching for Love 265

Search and Rescue 269
Being With You 271
Love's Call 273
Stand Still 275
Loneliness 277
Humanity's Heart 278
Being Invisible 279

Finding Love 281
One Thought of You 282
In Your Eyes 284
The Rescue 285
The Worthiest Goal 287
Why? 288
Ducks in a Row 289
The Fortress 290
Your Mercy 291
Love Realized 292
Our Synergy 294
Steppingstones 295

Erotica 297
Higher Love 302
The Dichotomy 303
All that You Are 304
Interplay 305
Guiding Star 306
Under the Moon 307
Battered Goddess 308
Calling Your Name 310
Love's Pursuit 311
Rising Up to Meet You 312
Stark Truth 314
Eternity's Gate 315
Reminder 316

Complete Me *317*
Healing Goddess *318*

Postscript 319
Index 329

To Marvin Schneider. I dedicate this book and my life to you. Thank you for being the co-author of my purpose. Without your kindness, support, patience, and genius, I may never have been seen or heard in this world. You are the embodiment of greatness realized. The synergy of our love is a key to opening the floodgates of higher consciousness. May the world see you through my eyes and heart.

There is nothing that a pure heart supported by a pure intention cannot accomplish.

—JEN WARD

Foreword

IT IS SUCH AN HONOR to write the foreword and chapter introductions to Jen Ward's collection of poems. This book, and the many more to come from the Jenuine Healing archives, reflect the true synergy between Jen and I in our intention to bring higher consciousness to all of humanity.

In this foreword, I will introduce Jen, her work, and our synergy in working together. It will provide some context to the poems and our intentions through these writings. The various chapter introductions will be my attempt, such as it is, to summarize the core spiritual principles and understandings that Jen shares with the world.

This book is more than just a collection of poems. We are excited to also include in this work, a collection of Jen's drawings, paintings, craftwork, and photos. These add to the already rich insights and messages conveyed in the poems themselves. Anyone who knows of Jen and her work will quickly appreciate that these images convey the energy and outpouring of her love and pure intention for every soul.

A good place to start this journey is to tell the story of how Jen and I first connected, and how we shortly thereafter came together as the embodiment of soul mates across all of time and space.

I have been on a path of spiritual discovery since about 2013. I was in my mid-forties at the time. The 'holy shit' moment came as I was doing some research on the internet and then randomly came across an old Youtube video on Pleiadean beings and their intention for humanity. It was an audio book reading of the book entitled 'Bringers of the Dawn' by Barbara Marciniak. That Youtube clip piqued my curiosity and set me on a journey of discovery.

Over the years, I found, absorbed, and practiced many forms of spiritual teachings. Meditation, yoga, chanting, and reading the wisdom of various enlightened Gurus was part of my daily practice.

From time to time, I got some inspiration from Darryl Anka and Lee Carrol who channel Bashar and Kryon respectively. I really liked the way Matt Kahn both entertained and enlightened his audiences. And from time to time, I would check in with what Pamela Aaralyn was sharing with the world. Each of these intuitive people have a large social media following through which they are able to connect with their audience.

It was on a cold Australian winter's day in mid July 2020 that I decided to check in with Pamela Aaralyn's Youtube channel again. She had just posted an interview with Jen entitled 'Become Your Own Healer.' As the interview began, probably after about the first couple of minutes, I remember saying to myself, 'holy shit, this chick is the real deal!'

During the interview, Jen came across as totally left field, quirky, passionate, but entirely coming from a position of pure intention, love and service to humanity. Her backstory and insights really resonated with me. Her SFT tapping technique struck me as a much more practical method of releasing core issues than mediation, chanting, breathing or other traditional spiritual practices that I had come to know in my journey. I was hooked.

I began listening to a few audio recordings of Jen's private sessions with clients. They were raw and confronting. There was a lot of grunting, screaming, and other noises which would be highly disconcerting to many people. It certainly was to me in the beginning. But I soon came to realize that these are the things that make Jen unique in her ability to heal her clients and release their core issues. She truly is a 'bad ass in energy.'

I went on Jen's website within a day or so of watching the Youtube interview to book my own private session. She was fully booked for six weeks in advance. So, every day while waiting for my private session, I listened to hours and hours of recorded private sessions. I must have listened to more than 120 recordings of private sessions over those six weeks. They covered the full gamut of the human experience – the good, the bad, and the ugly. I discovered pain and trauma that people suffer on a daily basis that I have thankfully not been exposed to. A lot of it was difficult to listen to.

But as I continued to listen and tap along with the clients, I experienced firsthand how Jen is able to zero in on the client's core issues and skillfully remove them with the compassion and intensity that only Jen is capable of. I witnessed how Jen confronts and deals with curses, possession, and entities as nothing more than stagnant energy that needs to be moved on.

I quickly got the memo on the dos and don'ts of how Jen likes to operate in her private sessions. She is very much the facilitator and healer, and you are the client. Don't talk too much - Jen doesn't want to hear your stuff. She'll know exactly what you need. Don't swear! From time-to-time Jen will use words with a harsh vibration to remove stagnant energy. But that is not an invitation for you to swear. Don't feel bad when you mess up the taps. It is a sign that the taps are dead on in addressing a core issue. Don't write stuff down while she's talking! That is disrespectful. Don't use long drawn out 'ums and ahs' That is also disrespectful in energy because it holds the other person captive in your sound frequency. Jen is going to ask you why you wanted a session with her. So, think about your answer beforehand – but keep it short and give your answer without dumping all your issues onto her.

These are just of few of the dos and don'ts that I locked onto by listening to other people's mistakes. So, for any of you who are reading this and are drawn to have your first private session with Jen – you are welcome!

While I was waiting for my private session, I downloaded the Energetic Cleanse and Peanut Butter & Jelly tapping protocols from Jen's website and compiled a list of issues or things that I wanted to release or remove from my energy field. It was a long list. I did two or three hours of tapping every day.

As the day of my session was drawing near, I checked in with Jen to confirm the date and time of the session because of the time zone differences between New York state and Australia. She texted back saying, 'you have good energy.' I was thinking something like, 'sure, I bet you say that to all your clients before a session.' She also asked me if I had done any tapping as preparation. I responded that I have done so many taps that I am bald on the top of my head. She gave me a 'lol' in the responding text.

I have always been a prolific dreamer. I have no issues getting to sleep and always wake up motivated and refreshed. But I have very vivid dreams. Many of them seem to go on for hours and hours. The scenes, the people, the smells, and the colors are all very vivid and all very real to me at the time. But the scenario, the premise or the canvas of the dreams often have an element of absurdity to them. The best way I can describe the absurd nature of many of my dreams is to compare them to scenes in a movie with a freakshow style carnival as a backdrop – you know, the ones that have warped mirrors and mazes with clowns and other freakish characters?

There were several occasions leading up to my private session that I had vivid dreams that featured Jen and me. They were all very intimate in nature. I saw Jen as the university professor and me as her favorite student. But the scenarios always went well beyond a typical student-teacher relationship. As much as I knew that Jen was helping me in my spiritual journey, I knew that I was helping Jen reconnect to the physical part of the human experience through intimacy. This was the first inkling I had of the synergy between me and Jen.

The private session itself was relatively uneventful. Of course, we did a lot of taps together, and of course Jen gave me a lot of homework. It was certainly not the confronting type of private session that I had experienced when listening to the audio recording of over a hundred other private sessions.

Perhaps the most interesting thing about my private session was that at the end, Jen asked me to stay on the call and 'chit chat' with her for a while. This was highly unusual. I have never heard Jen previously ask a client to 'chit chat'. It took me by surprise. We talked about the weather, some fun facts about Australia, and other things of no consequence. I was in two minds as to whether I should tell Jen about my dreams. I did, and Jen cried when I told her. I felt like such an asshole for making her cry on our first interaction.

So, that was that. Weeks went by. I continued to go through my homework. I became quite skilled at tapping and began to understand the more subtle aspects of Jen's SFT tapping protocols. I continued to spend hours per day listening to private session audio recordings. And I continued to have dreams of Jen.

I don't now recall how it came about, but we started texting each other on Facebook Messenger in the usual inconsequential 'bing-bang' style. This became all too much and was very exhausting. So, one day Jen asked if we could chat via audio, which we did. And soon after that, Jen asked if we could chat via video, which we did. We talked about a lot of unimportant things. And then one day I had another dream.

In this dream, I was a student in a very large lecture hall on my first day of university. There was not a spare seat in the house. I was sitting in the back row. I found this to be very unusual, because when I was at university, I was that annoying student sitting in the front row asking all the hard and inconvenient questions. Seated at the front of the theatre were all the professors in their full academic gowns. Jen was one of those professors.

The premise of the dream was that the professors chose their students and their course of study. I wanted to go into an engineering or science field of study. But I was disappointed when I was not chosen for these. Then it was Jen's turn to select her students for a degree in spirituality. Jen walked amongst the rows of prospective students until she reached the back row where I was seated. She stopped behind me, sniffed around my collar region, straightened herself up, and declared, 'this is the one!'

I told Jen of this dream. We both thought it was prescient. From that time on, Jen and I would have regular hours-long video conferences in which she would share with me her spiritual wisdom and insights, and I would ask the hard and inconvenient questions. I guess some things never change!

During those early months of interaction, we also did a lot of energy work to help me and my business partner at the time break through the resistance of communicating our ideas to potential clients. As much as this was work for Jen, I found out later that she liked to do it because it gave her an excuse to connect with me. For the record, Jen didn't much like or trust my business partner. More on that topic later.

During our more casual conversations, we talked about Australia, its nuances, animals, expressions, and attitudes. I told her about my intention to set up a working farm where paying clients would experience the farm life, enjoy a truly 'paddock to plate' dining experience, and attend business related workshops. She immediately recognized this as being in synergy with her intention to set up the Jenuine Healing Forest as a spiritual sanctuary for people to reconnect with the wisdom of the trees. Through this interaction and some of my dreams, we quickly realized that we had a synergy of purpose and that we were destined to be together. But in what form?

During one of our spiritual university sessions, Jen told me about her past life experience as Morgana (also known to some as the Lady of the Lake) in the King Arthur of Camelot lifetime. Her telling of the story was quite different from the characters and events that are often depicted in popular literature and cinema.

In her telling of the story, Morgana was the extremely spiritually advanced Goddess that was a half-sister to Arthur; that despite her genetic proximity to Arthur, Morgana was destined to marry him and rule with him for the purpose of uplifting all of humanity; that Merlin was not as capable a wizard as is generally thought; that Arthur's enchantment towards Guinevere was a spell destined to interrupt Arthur and Morgana's true purpose; that Lancelot was the ultimate villain that brought down Camelot through his affair with Guinevere; that as a result of this betrayal, Morgana was banished from Camelot; and that these sorry events prevented Camelot from fulfilling it's true purpose. Humanity was kept in the dark ages and the universal grand plan for an era of Lemurian style spiritual enlightenment was foiled – much to the displeasure of the Adepts.

So, at this stage, I should probably lay out the back story to the whole Arthur saga. My business partner at the time thought he was spiritually aware and had years of Eastern yogic practices under his belt. He convinced himself that he was a person of the Light that was battling the Dark. This narrative played out over the two or more decades that I was working with him.

He would often consult an energy worker in Australia to assist him in his 'battle against the Dark.' I had met this energy worker on several occasions and discovered through him that I had several past lives that involved me, my business partner, a young Chinese Australian woman that we employed for a while, and several historically well-known nefarious characters.

My then business partner was convinced that in one notable lifetime – being the Arthur lifetime - that he was Lancelot, I was his son Galahad, the Chinese Australia woman was Guinevere, the energy worker he consulted was Merlin, and the nefarious characters were opposing war lords.

When I relayed this to Jen, she immediately and emphatically stated that I was not Galahad in that lifetime. I was Arthur. It was our destiny to rule together and usher in a new era of human enlightenment. Lancelot was the destroyer of that destiny and the cause of Morgana being banished from Camelot. And that banishment sent Jen into nine centuries of traumatic and tragic lifetimes separated from her soulmate – me!

This explains why Jen had such a negative reaction to my business partner. She explained that he was not a person of the Light at all. His primary purpose in all the lives that we have incarnated together was to capture and entangle me to prevent me from realizing myself as an incarnated Adept whose purpose was to usher humanity into a new era of spiritual enlightenment. The Arthur lifetime was just one of several attempts by the Adepts to bring mass enlightenment to Earth.

Now I don't know about you, but that is a lot for a country lad from Australia to absorb in one go.

And so now Jen and I are realized soul mates that have reconnected after at least nine centuries to continue the work and purpose that we have always been destined to manifest for the benefit of all of humanity. Although we have a shared purpose to uplift all of humanity, we each do it in very different ways.

Jen is focused on applying her energy healing and medical intuitive capabilities to help individuals address core issues and remove stagnant energy so that they can realize their purpose and be the best expression of themselves as possible. I have myself witnessed the profound impact of her work by viewing the recordings of hundreds of private healing sessions. And these are just a small sample of the more than 1,000 healing sessions that Jen has facilitated since 2009.

A core aspect of Jen's work with clients during private sessions is her use of the SFT tapping protocols that she was guided to develop by the Adepts. Her book *The SFT*

Lexicon: Second Edition is an excellent reference book in the construction and use of SFT tapping protocols.[1] I thoroughly recommend this book to you. It will quickly become your 'go to' textbook for achieving a purpose-led, fulfilled, and transcended life.

Over the months that we interacted during the early days, Jen has told me about the tragic circumstances of her upbringing in this life, and the many tragic and traumatic lives she had experienced since her banishment by me. You truly would not wish those experienced onto anyone. But as we talk about them, we saw a pattern of conditioning and scenarios that the Adepts have helped orchestrate that have allowed Jen to be so effective in her work. It has afforded her an ability to identify with, understand, and have compassion for, the full range of experiences that we often describe as 'the human condition.' What is amazing to me is that despite all of this, Jen still has an infinite capacity to love all life – both animate and inanimate.

I think it is worth attempting to describe, such as it is, my interpretation of what Jen does in her work, and how she does it.

Through some process that I still do not fully understand, Jen is highly attuned to perceiving in energy. I suspect that this capability has been developed over many lifetimes because of her being sensory deprived of 'normal' physical human experiences. Or maybe it is the case that Jen has been sensory deprived from these experiences because she is hypersensitive to perceiving in energy. Either way, what I do know is that Jen's ability to perceive in energy is off the scale. It allows her to do three important things.

---

[1] You can purchase of copy of The SFT Lexicon: Second Edition at https://jenuinehealing.com/product/the-sft-lexicon-second-edition/

The first is to be in an almost constant state of dialogue with the Adepts through which she gets information, insights, and nudges to do things. Think about this as an ability to tap into direct knowingness, consciously and effortlessly. A lot of people access direct knowingness in their dream state or through mediation. But Jen can access this at will.

The second is that when she tunes into the energy field of her clients during private sessions, she can immediately 'see' past-life engrams that are creating blockages to the client realizing perpetual joy, love, abundance, freedom, health, success, security, companionship, creativity, peace, life, wholeness, beauty, enthusiasm, contentment, spirituality, enlightenment, confidence, empowerment, sincerity, integrity, imagination, and kindness.

But for me, the most important thing is Jen's ability to assist in removing engrams and moving stagnant energy out of the client's sound frequency and light emanation. It is one thing for clients to utilize Jen's SFT tapping protocols on their own. But it is infinitely more powerful to do so with Jen's assistance during private sessions. If you have not yet had a private session with Jen, I thoroughly recommend you do so.[2]

My contribution to the upliftment of all of humanity is to lead the transformation of the global business and investment communities to create wealth on an ongoing basis in ways that enhance societal wellbeing. This purpose is grounded in a noble intent to bring the global business and investment communities into higher consciousness. There is a lot of work to be done to realize this purpose. This is because most of the business and investment

---

[2] You can book a private session with Jen at https://jenuinehealing.com/product/jenuine-healing-session/

community members currently operate with a high degree of self-interest and indifference as to the impact of their activities on individuals, the wider community, and the environment. Be sure to read the Postscript at the end of this book for more about my work in transforming the global business and investment communities.

A key aspect of the transformation of companies and investment firms is to shift those in leadership roles to operate from a position of higher consciousness. This is where Jen and I are connected in synergy of purpose. We are currently developing and rolling out a series of workshops aimed at corporate professionals involved in the 'people side' of business. These workshops will help them enhance their skills to perceive in energy, access higher consciousness, tap into direct knowingness, and utilize SFT tapping techniques in their own professional careers. Having these skills will significantly amp up the capabilities and effectiveness of people operating in professional senior corporate careers.

Aside from these things, there are several other ways that Jen and I are working together in collaboration.

The Jenuine Healing brand was renewed and refreshed in January 2021 to incorporate design elements from the Australian outback. This reflects our intention to make Australia a global focal point of higher consciousness. You can see those branding elements on the Jenuine Healing website and all of Jen's other social media outlets listed on page xxvii.

Every now and then, and particularly on key portal dates, either Jen or I get a nudge to schedule an 'uplifting all of humanity' group SFT tapping session. We generally get between 20-30 people from all over the world participating in these group SFT tapping sessions. There is something magical about having a large group of people with pure intentions putting energy into the collective at the same time. Some of the more recent group tapping sessions have addressed issues such as healing Australia; breaking down forever-chemicals; dissipating social divisiveness; helping those that are lost and lonely during the holiday season; reversing climate change; breaking up digital monopolies; dissipating nefarious intentions; healing the wounds of September 11; and many, many more. You can sign up to the email newsletter on the Jenuine Healing website to receive notifications of future free group SFT tapping events designed to uplift all of humanity.

And of course, I would be seriously remiss if I did not give proper attention in this foreword to the *Jen in her Jammies* podcast series that is published on Youtube and many other podcast outlets. Anyone who doesn't know about the *Jen in her Jammies* podcast series has clearly been living under a rock.

By way of background, I should mention that I have been an extremely private person for most of my life. So, it came as quite a surprise to me when I had a dream one night in February 2021 in which Jen and I were hosting a podcast. When I told Jen about the dream, she immediately was onboard with the idea. I was hesitant and resisted acting on the dream. But then I did some research on podcasting, the equipment you need, and how to edit videos. We designed a thumbnail image, found some introduction music, and started thinking about the format of our podcast. We settled on *Jen in her Jammies* as the name of the podcast and recorded the pilot episode on March 15, 2021.[3]

The premise of *Jen in her Jammies* is to highlight and play on the fact the Jen and I represent polar opposites on

---

[3] You can view the pilot episode of *Jen in her Jammies* by going onto Youtube and typing '*Jen in her Jammies* pilot episode' into the Youtube search bar.

almost all dimensions. I represent the left-brained, conservative, analytical, and mainstream of society dressed in smart business casual clothing. Jen represents the right-brained, unconventional, free spirit part of society dressed in her pajamas and featuring an array of plushies. Yet despite our polar opposite nature, we come together in mutual love and respect to explore spiritual and healing topics in a lighthearted manner.

I sometimes think that a lot of people tune into new episodes to keep up to date with the *Jen in her Jammies* plushy family. Many of our listeners eagerly follow the lives and activities of Darshan, Gunter, Little Jen, Albert, Jordan and Tristan. Over time, the plushy family has grown to include Ozgood, Kiwi, Kip, Gumby, Lambsie, Magda, Manfred, Baby Jordan, Baby Tristan, and a gaggle of squirrels, chipmunks and shrimps. Each one of the plushies have their own personality, roles and relationships. For example, Gunter and Little Jen are an item; Ozgood is in an interspecies relationship with Kiwi; Darshan and Kip are best friends, and Darshan has his own wife and bear offspring; and Albert has a wife and koala offspring. You have no idea how active the plushies are!

The plushies play a significant role in the *Jen in her Jammies* podcast series. They provide healing energy to the listener. Jen uses the plushies to teach people to communicate with the inanimate world to enhance their abilities to perceive in energy. And they represent a permission slip for people to reconnect with their inner child. This is important because children are highly intuitive, creative, and can easily access direct knowingness. Society bleeds these innate capabilities from us through the education system, cultural conditioning, and a perception that you need to be tough, analytical and a conformist to be successful in a corporate career.

In the early days of *Jen in her Jammies*, I would plan each episode meticulously and script a series of bullet points to guide the conversation in a structured way. I quickly realized that Jen cannot be scripted. She totally operates in the moment. Nowadays, we just set up the recording studio, hit the record button, and pray that the listener will get some benefit and healing from whatever transpires between the beginning and end of the recording.

We receive a lot of encouraging comments from our audience, both as comments on the Youtube clip itself, and in private emails to Jen. It seems that as goofy and oddball many of the episode are, people are still keen to tune in and connect with the *Jen in her Jammies* family. We have had quite a few people tell us that their day is brightened just by listening to the latest episode. We are so grateful for all the support we receive and encourage as many people as possible to share this valuable resource so that other people can be healed and can have an opportunity to have their own 'holy shit' moment when they first meet Jen.

More recently, Jen and I are collaborating to update and edit many of her 19 books. There is so much wisdom and practical guidance contained in Jen's books. We now have the luxury of time to work our way through the material contained in the collection of Jen's books and package it so that it is even more accessible to a wider audience.

I recommend this book to you. I trust that it will take pride of place on your coffee table to be appreciated daily.

Marvin Schneider
Wodonga, Australia
March 2022

Jenuine Healing on Social Media

JENUINE HEALING has an active social media presence in order to bring higher consciousness and healing into the mainstream. Here are some links to Jenuine Healing's various social media channels.

Website: https://jenuinehealing.com
Purchase: https://jenuinehealing.com/purchase/
Books: https://jenuinehealing.com/books-2/
Youtube: https://youtube.com/jenuinehealing
Podcast: https://anchor.fm/jenuinehealing
LinkedIn: https://www.linkedin.com/in/jenuinehealing
Facebook: https://www.facebook.com/jen.ward.984/
Twitter: https://twitter.com/jenuinehealing

CHAPTER 1

Universal Consciousness

MORE AND MORE PEOPLE are contemplating the really big questions as every day goes by. What is the nature of universal consciousness? What is the meaning of life? Why does Life exist at all? And what is our role in the grand design of the universe, such as it is?

Unfortunately, there are still billions of people on the planet that have either never contemplated these questions or are resolute in the idea that there is no higher purpose at all. For them, life is all about getting as much as possible for themselves during their short tenure on Earth, even if it is achieved at the expense of others. Greed, the accumulation of wealth and power, self-interest, and indifference are their tools of trade. If you are at this end of the spectrum, perhaps these writings will give you a moment of pause and trigger within you the kind of 'holy shit' moment that seems to be common to all those awakening.

Then there are the billions of people who have a sense of some form of universal consciousness, but who are captive to the dogma surrounding mainstream religions or other forms of spiritual practice. This entrapment holds them in lower consciousness and prevents them from realizing themselves as omniscient, omnipresent, and omnipotent beings. It is what Jen calls being trapped in the 'daisy of death.' If you are in this predicament, perhaps these writings may give you an opportunity to subtly shift vantage point and reclaim your sovereignty.

In this chapter introduction, I will attempt to lay out, as best as I understand it, the nature of universal consciousness and our role in its grand design. My understanding of these things is heavily influenced by the many hours of spiritual tutelage provided by Jen as guided through her by the Adepts. As I gingerly navigate my way through these heady topics, I fully acknowledge that I do not have all the answers. I have become comfortable with the idea that there are some mysteries of the universe that will remain a mystery to me for as long as I choose to incarnate in a physical form.

While I am open to a lot of alternative modes of thinking, at the end of the day, I am a very practical person. I get frustrated when reading the wise words and counsel of gurus, sages, ascended masters and the like that are written in riddles. So, I have constructed what I consider to be the core tenets of higher consciousness and spirituality in plain English as follows:

- there is a universal consciousness – we will call it Source to avoid drawing upon the tainted concept of God;

- we are spiritual beings whose consciousness exists beyond a single incarnated life. Most people alive on Earth right now have had many hundreds or thousands of incarnated lives – not all of which have played out on Earth;

- as spiritual beings, we are an aspect of Source, and are interconnected with everything in the universe – both animate and inanimate;

- all individual atoms of Source possess awareness, and are therefore conscious;
- the purpose of an individual's life in its incarnated form is to realize itself as a conscious being in its relationship to all other conscious beings;
- the purpose of Life in its broadest perspective is to perceive life from every possible vantage point as a means to move the collective closer to Source;
- the base nature of Source is love;
- gratitude and enthusiasm are the doorways to higher consciousness, whereas regret and apathy shut down opportunity; and
- the journey towards and beyond enlightenment never ends.

These core tenets speak to our identity as spiritual beings that are an aspect of Source having a human experience for the purpose of expanding universal consciousness; and in the process, realizing ourselves as being an aspect of Source by piercing through the veil of separation that descends upon incarnation. Simple, right?

I think of Source as the primordial energy of the universe that is constantly in a state of flux, and which is perpetually organizing and reorganizing itself in ways that create experiences, memories, and imprints within the fabric of the totality of all the energy contained within the universe. This process adds to the consciousness of the universe.

I find it helpful to think of the origin of the universe as emanating from the big bang. The big bang is that instant in time when all the energy that is and ever will be in the universe was ushered into physical existence. Since the time of the big bang, that energy has formed and transformed itself to create everything that is observable in the universe.

That means every atom that is observable in the universe has been transmuted from all the energy contained in the big bang.

And it gets more interesting. It is increasingly accepted that the universe we are currently experiencing as a result of its big bang is not the first big bang to have ever occurred, nor will it be the last. In fact, there is a view that we are currently experiencing the 84th incarnation of the physical universe. In this sense, the universe ebbs and flows, and creates and stores consciousness throughout it various journeys. But even within the 84th incarnation of the universe, there are still echoes of consciousness from the more recent previous incarnations.

Is there an intelligence responsible for each of the big bangs? Is there some kind of grand planner that orchestrates all that is in the macrocosm within each universe and between the universal ebbs and flows? To be honest, I have no idea. I know that various Hindu traditions give credence to Shiva filling this role, in which he brings about the destruction of one universe and 'roars' to usher in the big bang creation of the next universe.

I find it helpful to understand Source and the universe in terms of acquired consciousness rather than an orchestrating intelligence. This is because it fits more naturally with the subtleties of the remaining tenets in which the purpose of Life is to expand the consciousness of the universe through experiences. It fits more naturally within the notion of free will and the exploration of souls in the universe as part of a pathway back to Source.

Of course, I am willing to concede that my conception of Source may be wrong. For what it is worth, I do not find it practically helpful to explore the topic at a deeper level. I put this question in the category of the mysteries of the universe that will remain a mystery to me. In any case, there is enough richness in my current understanding to keep me busy for all the lives in which I chose to incarnate in the playground of this, the 84th universe.

For me, the most profound realization is that we are all spiritual beings that are an aspect of Source having a human experience. Jen often describes us as being an emanation of light and a frequency of sound woven together in the illusion of form. In this sense, we are first and foremost energy. The trick for us having an incarnated human experience is to recognize ourselves as such. This is a really hard thing to do for most people. This is because most of us have very tangible experiences in the physical realm. To suggest that the physical world is an illusion seems absurd to many people.

I am sure there are some highly enlightened souls on Earth that can primarily experience themselves as energy in which the physical realm is an illusion. A guru sitting in the lotus position in a perpetual state of meditation may be an example of this phenomenon. I know that Jen spends a lot of her time connected to Source in energy. I suspect that is why it is difficult for her to be grounded in the physical realm. And I suspect that other people that are more attuned to their energy body also find it very difficult to function in the physical world.

For my part, I do not deny the human experience I am having. I am heavily grounded in the physical realms. I do not think I will ever be able to fully comprehend the illusory nature of matter, time, and space. In some ways, I am glad of that because it allows me to fully function in the physical realm.

And while there are some subtleties of the universe that are simply beyond my comprehension, acknowledging that we are all interconnected with everything in the universe is profoundly important for the way we live our lives. Our one job in life is to lift the veil of separation that descends upon incarnation and realize ourselves as an aspect of Source connected to 'all that is' in the universe.

The poems and artwork that follow in this chapter explore various aspects of the nature of universal consciousness and our purpose of recognizing ourselves as an aspect of Source. I trust that they will inspire you to either begin your own spiritual journey or to ground you in your existing journey.

Marvin Schneider
Wodonga, Australia
March 2022

May All Blessings Be

Any arms are my arms
That reach out to hug
Whether they represent a saint
Or belong to a thug.

Any pain is my pain
It all cuts so deep
I feel internal angst
Am compelled just to weep.

Any life is a value
So worth taking up space
The divine act of existing
An immense act of grace.

Every soul has a vantage point
So worth the knowing
By exploring its depth
Enacts our own growing.

Any heart is a heart
Well worth the beating
It's best to engage in life
Than be always defeating.

Every life is valuable
Especially your own
Enlightening yourself
Is living in the zone.

You are valued and respected
A Being of pure light
Recognizing your empowerment
Brings the world new delight.

What you choose to do
With this expression that is you
Teaches the whole world
What it is able to do.

The more you embrace your greatness
With a kindness and a grace
The more easily this world becomes
An enlightened loving place.

In fact, the whole world at large
Is a reflection of you
So for the sake of all life
Love everything you do.

Stand by what you say
The truth that you command
The fate of the world
Sits squarely in your hand.

When you emanate with love
Wherever you may go
You are feeding eternal love
To all those who don't know.

So, for the grace of humanity
The collective We
May you be a blessing to all
And may all blessings Be.

The Fight

I am a devoted champion of love
If only in my own mind
I dig the trenches and dutifully fight
In ruthless defense to be kind.

I undo the damage that's been done
From each powerful selfish decree
I heal the wounds of all that suffer
Or perhaps just the suffering in me.

I can't condone the apathy of Man
As displayed in ignorance's defense
I can only abide bullshit so long
Or condone systemic pretense.

I will continue to serve others as I do
How else could I possibly endure
Someone must heal the ills of all men
Until each Being finds its own cure.

The Apathy of Man

Who I am is not forged
In flesh or words or pride
Who I am is drawn much deeper
From the ethereal world I reside.

Who I am is not crushed
By mock or scorn or slight
Whatever devastates the external me
Melts away through celestial flight.

Who I am reminds all others
They live beyond mortal stone
Who they are runs much deeper
Than the trespasses for which they atone.

You and I are not the script
In which we were given at birth
You and I are absolute truth
Joy, love, abundance, and mirth.

You and I are angelic captains
Navigating a sea of Sound and Light
Whatever realities we conjure up
Melt away through our second sight.

You and I have co-created
This illusion we are living in
We have all co-written the storyboard
Of hate and greed and sin.

Yet, no matter how long we have endured
It's not too hard to see
When we wince and wipe the crust from our eyes
What we envision always comes to be.

You and I as creative beings
Have been given a new task
To crumple old blueprints of this world
Strip power of its walls and masks.

Create a new vision of a new Earth
Where all are equal and free
The love and the light of our true home
Will be written in this new Earth's decree.

This one small task is entrusted to us
The awakening of a new realm
You and I are co-creators
Responsible for steering the helm.

You and I must show the whole world
Through kindness, beauty, and truth
The world they once envisioned
In the reckless days of their youth.

You and I have emerged from the mist
There is no use trying to go back
We have agreed to show all other souls
The love and joy they have lacked.

This is an exciting time of being
An alchemy in which we partake
To transform the marauding apathy of Man
As we heal all those in its wake.

Pure Love

I am a crystal
I am a tree
I am a poet
I am a bee.

I am the ocean
I am each wave
I am life's troubadour
Its unbridled knave.

I am the sunshine
That luminates the sea
I am the moonbeam
I dance upon me.

I am whatever experience
I gratefully allow
I am the farmer
I am the plow.

I move through each atom
From below and above
I am capable of all this
Because I am pure love.

A State of Being

The unequivocal distinction
Between thinking and knowing
The symbiotic relationship
Between coming and going.

The melodic precision
Of a satisfying resound
Commanding a presence
Without uttering a sound.

A defining conjecture
That becomes a decree
Obeying it faithfully
Are we really free?

Incredible grace
While being under fire
The fortitude it takes
To fulfill any desire.

The dancing arrangement
Of atoms of air
Questioning inconsistencies
That aren't really there.

Being is being
Either close or afar
We all belong somewhere
Wherever we are.

Perceiving in Energy

You see an acorn
I see a tree
You make random statements
I hear a decree.

You shed a tear
I see resolve
You feel the pain
I help it dissolve.

You're counting down
To a final hour
I serve an infinite world
I strive to empower.

You diminish the world
With your careless dismissal
Creating a world
That is fearful and abysmal.

The God that you pray to
Is not up in the sky
It's in the face of your brethren
Toe to toe, eye to eye.

When you are kind, thoughtful, caring
Your countenance is true
Goodness works through your intention
And all that you do.

You're awakening to empowerment
Striving for peace for us all
Hear the music of nature
Answer it's call.

Swim through the currents
That are graceful and kind
Speak well of all creatures
Unburden the mind.

Give better than you get
Religiously too
This is the empowerment
Awakening in you.

You are the seed
Of an amazing new realm
You navigate the ship
Your truth is the helm.

Speak and be it now
In confidence and insight
You are the love
You are the light.

> The Love that you give out,
> is an extension of your own hands.

Individuality

A grain of sand on the shore that catches the light
That one grounded bird that learns to take flight.

The unencumbered soul that unfurls to be free
That voice of dissension that learns to agree.

The infant who remembers what it's like to be old
A flame that reminds you what it is like to be cold.

Defeating lost hope by saying, 'I can'
Incarnating comfortably being woman or man.

Creating a symphony one note at a time
Knowing peace during chaos, however sublime.

The sliver of knowledge that turns into a wedge
Being pushed past all reason, jumping over the ledge.

There's no separation between the foam and the sea
Illusion's the only distinction between what's you and what's me.

> No, I am NOT a Dog
>
> I am a person of the canine persuasion
>
> jenuinehealing.com

Balance

I am a windfall
I am a tree
I am everything that comes
So sweetly to be.

I am a rainfall
I am a drought
I dry up all adversity
Then pour myself out.

I am the wildfires
Burning out of control
They indeed have a purpose
They too have a role.

I burn up negativity
Then chill myself out
I am the fire hose
I put myself out.

I am every child
Who is fleeing from war
Their life has a purpose
With more to explore.

I am the soldier
Who wraps innocence in wire
The fear in their heart
Caused by political mire.

I am the calm
When one is laid to their rest
Know they've given their all
And just did their best.

Being Present

The intersection of time and space
Where yin and yang agree
Everything and nothing collide
In a blind spot they can't see.

Where alpha and omega merge
Where true knowingness can actually be
A random someone meets their true self
To realize they are already free.

There is a particular perspective
Like the pinnacle of a hill
Everything comes into focus
Perpetual motion becomes still.

Where universal law
Bends to the bias of no decree
The wonders of joy, love, and abundance
Are as affluent as can be.

You become the windfall
In expansiveness beyond the mind
Existence is your bounty
In reconnecting with love's kind.

Love in the End

Solar flares
Winter blues
Indian summer
Déjà vu.

Quiet outbursts
Putting allegations to bed
Are we guided by angels
Or just randomly led?

Each season's solstice
Swimming up creek
Finding answers to questions
Dismissed by the meek.

Desiring to go further
Than your leash will allow
Finding God in all places
Even in worshiping a cow.

Searching all temples
Revisiting all shrines
Is your God the real one
Or is it mine?

Standing on a pulpit
Or shouting from the street
Find love in all places
Shake hands when you meet.

Nature or nurture
It's really a moot point
If you feel God's everywhere
Then he's there to anoint.

When your blood, brains, and bones
Are put into the ground
It's the You that is left
That still hovers around.

Ascends into heaven
Re-acclimates
Remembers it's been there
Revisits its fate.

It does it all over
Again and again
Until you realize each moment
That we're all love in the end.

A Portal of God

To dance upon the horizon all through the night
To live in the exhilaration of an eagle's first flight.

To pursue a purity all others abscond
To breathe in each moment, forever and beyond.

To dive into the heavens as your own private pool
To see life from the vantage point of a perpetual school.

To be the lover, the teacher, the healer of Man
Living in the moment where all ends and began.

To rise to the surface of humanity's cream
To support each being's purpose, their intimate dream.

To cheerlead all others and actually applaud
Is the moment you become a portal of God.

All Life

Heaven is not a place for me
With rules I must comply
God is not a man somewhere
On a throne up in the sky.

Source is an everlasting vigil
To balance out the soul
Align myself with the universe
In order to be made whole.

It's aligning all I am, feel, and think
In the experience of me
To resonate with the universe
Is to let myself be free.

Providence isn't an idea for me
Or somewhere out in space
It's a perpetual state of being
In service and in grace.

My quest to find Source
Embodies the struggle of every Man
Instead of taking anything from others
I give all that I can.

Heaven is sweet synchronicity
A balance if you will
Relinquishing the controlling mind
Just learning to be still.

The beauty of this heaven of mine
Is that there is no pass or fail
Just giving all you have to give
To help all life prevail.

Human Victory

There's a quiet inner place
Between hunger and being fed
That draws upon a stillness
To which we can't be led.

It's a spacious reverent moment
Between the exhale and the breath
When Man surmounts all limits
Explores an inner depth.

In this place of quiet reason
Well beyond the visceral mind
Humanity discovers a freedom
The brain alone can't find.

It can't be measured in human increments
Or expressed in words alone
We are coaxed by higher purpose
As petty transgressions are atoned.

Possibilities are endless
Beyond a linear latitude
It's a form of human victory
To know such gratitude.

CHAPTER 2

The Human Collective

THE MOST PROFOUND realization I had when embarking on my own spiritual journey was that we are all atoms of Source and eternals souls contained in energy having a myriad of incarnated experiences for the purpose of realizing ourselves as an aspect of Source.

This is profound because it helps me ponder my own life's purpose. Appreciating your life's purpose is one of the most vexing questions facing most of the 7.9 billion people living on this planet, let alone the endless number of other souls incarnated on the endless number of other lower worlds. This search for purpose is perhaps the one thing that binds us all as part of the human collective.

So, in this chapter introduction, I will explore several topics related to the human collective that are offshoots of the central theme of 'the veil of separation' that exists within the lower worlds.

As Jen describes it, the lower worlds are those which operate within the confines of the physical, astral, causal, and mental planes of existence. These are the planes of existence at which the ego operates. The etheric plane is beyond the ego and is the gateway into the higher worlds. The higher worlds are well beyond the ego, and in which the veil of separation no longer exists.

The four planes of existence that represent the lower worlds operate at different vibratory rates. For example, Jen describes the astral plane as being so close in vibration to the physical plane that a lot of people find it difficult to perceive the difference between them. Yet they are different in energy. And the laws of physics that govern these planes are somewhat different.

For example, within the physical plane of existence, the laws of physics as we know them regulate the interaction and relationship between energy, matter, gravity, time, and space. On this plane of existence, we perceive time as linear, and we are bound by the laws of gravity. But on the astral plane, which is very close in energetic proximity to the physical plane, we can move more freely in time and space, and we are easily able to engage in astral travel beyond the confines of gravity.

The four planes of existence that define the lower worlds are very harsh in vibration relative to the higher worlds. When we incarnate into the lower worlds, we are bound by the limiting laws of physics that govern the lower worlds. These laws of physics create the veil of separation that descends upon us at the point of incarnation.

Jen often says that it is more difficult and traumatic to be born than it is to die. This makes a lot of sense to me. Upon death as I understand it, the soul's consciousness is passed back to the astral body and is engaged in a review process within the astral plane. It is free from the constraints of the physical realm. Upon being reborn into the lower worlds, the soul is reintroduced to the laws of physics and limitations of the physical plane of existence. Part of the soul's consciousness is trapped within the mind of a new body and is separated from the collective consciousness. The veil of separation has once again descended. I can understand why this is a very lonely and traumatic experience.

Which begs an obvious question. Why on earth would anyone reincarnate into the lower worlds, with all the attendant constraints in doing so if they have the free choice not to? Why not just continue to exist in a non-corporeal form within the astral, causal, and mental realms? Or even better, why don't we just transcend the lower worlds altogether, pierce through the membrane of the etheric plane, and glide into the realms of the higher worlds?

Jen and I spend a lot of time exploring these intriguing questions. Is it the case that 'the Lords of Karma' keep us trapped within an endless cycle of reincarnation into the worlds of duality, pain, and suffering? Do we have free will at all with respect to reincarnation?

The answers to these questions, as best as I can understand them, lie within a simple notion. There is a dominant and almost overpowering force within the universe that seeks to expand consciousness. It is like the underlying driving force that perpetuates life on Earth. Or the force that drives salmon to run the gauntlet of migrating upstream to spawn new life.

Universal consciousness expands through experiences. Experiences are best had within the course vibration and duality of the lower worlds. So, as much as it may be traumatic and lonely to reincarnate into the lower worlds under the veil of separation, the drive to do so for the purpose of expanding universal consciousness is so dominant that we reincarnate out of habit. It is part of our nature as eternal souls. And we tend to keep doing so until we have had all possible experiences in the lower worlds such that there is nothing more to add to universal consciousness from our continued reincarnation. It is at this point that we transcend the ego and glide through the membrane of the etheric plane into the higher worlds.

One of the cool things about Jen's work is that she is teaching humanity the pathway to actively choose whether they want to reincarnate into the lower worlds or not. And that pathway is to transcend the ego and recognize ourselves as omniscient, omnipresent, and omnipotent beings. At this point, we have the awareness of our choice to reincarnate, and do not simply do it out of habit.

I have also asked Jen whether souls originate from the higher worlds, and whether the Adepts only operate within the higher worlds. She explains that all souls originate from the higher worlds and soon after experience their first incarnation in the lower worlds. Once there, they tend to reincarnate into the lower worlds until such time as they transcend the ego and rejoin Source within the higher worlds. She also explained that the Adepts are able to freely navigate between the higher worlds and the lower worlds. Which explains why some Adepts choose the incarnate into the lower worlds for the purpose of assisting those beings 'trapped' in the lower worlds.

So, the veil of separation experienced by those souls 'trapped' in the lower worlds is one of the things that unite us as part of the human collective. We are all on a journey to realize ourselves as an atom of Source seeking to return to Source and transcend the lower worlds. The difficulty is that there are several aspects of the human experience that perpetuate the separation from Source and the human collective.

As if it is not bad enough that we incarnate into the lower worlds under the veil of separation, there are some things about the human experience and conditioning that perpetuate that sense of separation – both from Source and from the human collective. And that sense of separation then perpetuates the role played by the ego, duality, pain, suffering, the abuse of power, the loss of empowerment, and being trapped in the daisy of death. All these outcomes are still unfortunately a significant part of the human experience.

Fear is a powerful form of human and social conditioning. In the beginning of the human experience on Earth, fear was a useful survival mechanism within a harsh and hostile environment. But later, fear was used by tribal leaders to control the group and maintain tribal cohesion. With it came an 'us versus them' mentality. That level of tribalism is still evident today, and possibly even more pronounced in this age of social media and distrust of governments and other social institutions. Through it, we have lost our connection to the human collective and to Source.

Perhaps the most significant regression in consciousness away from a connection to the human collective and Source occurred when the concept of 'one life' was introduced into several mainstream religious belief systems. Why did this occur? Perhaps doing so elevated the status of religious leaders as a conduit to Source and served as a mechanism to control and influence the faithful. But in any case, it resulted in a significant disruption to a sense of connection to the human collective and to Source.

My own view is that a lot of the challenges we observe in the world today can only be resolved when a large proportion of the population regain their connection to the human collective and to Source, and in doing so, reclaim their empowerment as omniscient, omnipresent, and omnipotent beings.

So how do we do this in a world that operates under the veil of separation, and in which greed, self-interest and indifference is so prevalent? Jen's answer to this is to change your vantage point from taking to outflowing. When we outflow, we give back to humanity, the Earth, and the universe. Jen often says that the true gauge of how well we are plugged into the collective is our capacity to love others outside of ourselves. Perhaps our capacity to love our children and family members, despite all the challenges presented, is our training wheel for loving all in the collective.

The poems and artwork that follow in this chapter explore various aspects of the human collective. May they awaken your own connection to the human collective and to Source.

Marvin Schneider
Wodonga, Australia
March 2022

The Gift of This Life's Struggle

Beautiful statistic
A number on a page
Is this death count you contribute to
A valuable life gauge?

How many people did you love?
Did you serve, teach, or amuse?
Will all the good that you did here
Be dismissed with the next day's news?

What were your thoughts as you died alone?
Were you paralyzed in disbelief?
Did the inhumanity of your final breaths
Mean death brought some relief?

Were you loved and cared for?
Did you silently weep within?
Was a stranger's voice your comfort?
Did you lament death's cruel chagrin?

Dear one please realize
Wherever your body lay
Your life here still had purpose
Valued in an immeasurable way.

Can you forgive the ignorance
That led to your demise?
Can you love and show compassion
For those that society despise?

May the integrity that flows through you
Down to your tiniest finger
Permeate the densest of heart
Dissolve indifference that may linger.

May all that you endured
Not be thought of as a lost cause
But give those who live in apathy
A reason to take pause.

May they be grateful for their opportunity
To continue to share and grow
May they give a moment to reflect upon
What you already know.

That the gift of this life's struggle
Is a blessing we can't surpass
Loving life in the harshest conditions
Is a splendor in the grass.

Being in the hands of strangers
Who know little the life you have lived
Has a special value in the heaven you land
Granting access with no debt to forgive.

We may not know your sweet smile
Or the gentle caress of your hand
But your experience is added to the book of life
To help others to understand.

Walk away sweet traveler
In the hand of an angel of grace
We will miss your sweet presence
And the experience in the lines of your face.

These tears we shed for loved ones
Are now offered up to you
Your passing graces all of creation
As men learn from the indifference they do.

You are the whisper of simpler times
Our fate rests in the peace that you've won
Please know that your memory is etched in time
When the salvation of humanity has begun.

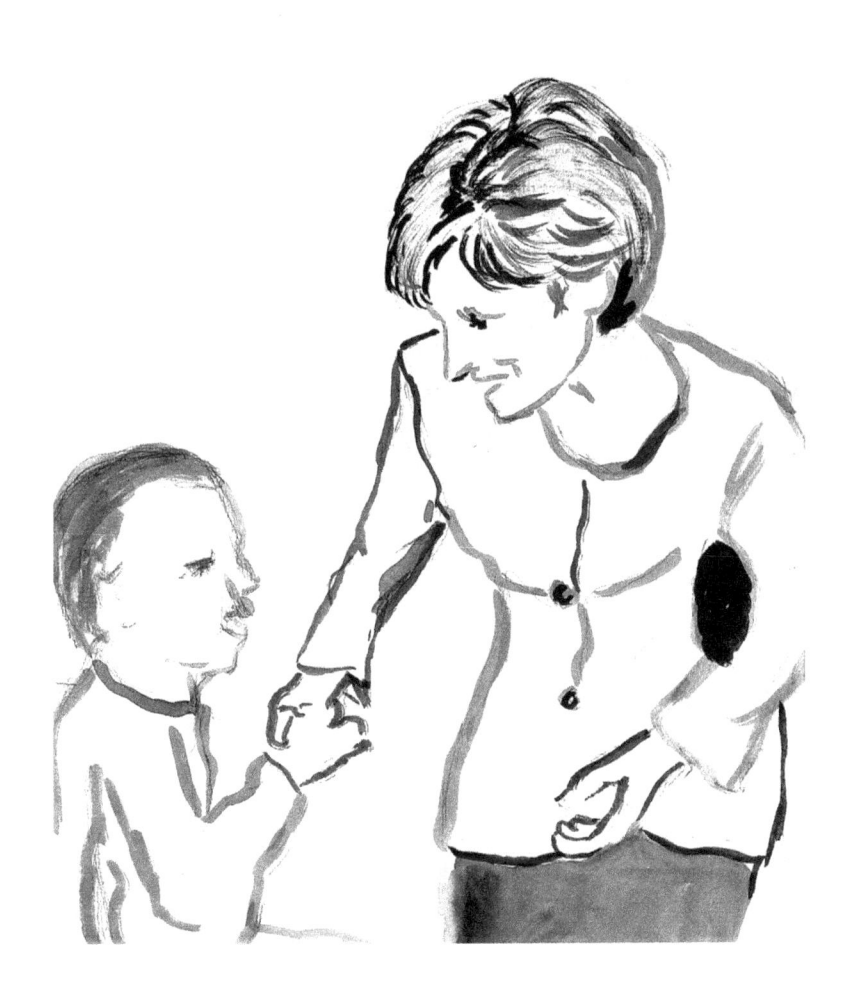

Second Sight

Cut away the blind spots
That choke your inner vision
Pain and loss are the site
Of the first incision.

Craving, want, hunger, and need
Expand the void in which we bleed
Feeding intentions to inspire
Dries a lustful wanton desire.

Pay the piper with true coin
Selfless goodness fill the void
As human nature wax and wane
Primal urges start to refrain.

Beyond the caliber of the night
Through the vestige of second sight
Partake of the world as it's meant to be
Illuminated, abundant, loving, and free.

Shadows Come Alive

Shadows come alive
When they catch my eye
They live within the crevices
Where promises go to die.

They hint of cruel realities
That aren't physically even there
They give legs, teeth, and voice
To everything I fear.

Shadows in my mind
Taunt me out of reach
How to move beyond them
Is something they don't teach.

So, I will put a spotlight
On every single one
Un-nestle them from their sanctuary
Where their hold on me begun.

You can slap a label on it
Medicate it to death
Deny it up the yin yang
Or drown it out with meth.

But to move beyond the shadows
Hold credence to all you do
Give breath, vision, form, and substance
To the greatest sense of you.

Humanity

When did I become invisible
Unable to be seen
When was the last time I caught a glimpse of myself
Without feeling so unclean

When was the last time I didn't feel shame
For merely being undressed
When was the last time I laid down my head
Without feeling such unrest

I am humanity personified
Gently walking amongst the crowd
Continuously striving to bring everyone love
Merely by speaking it out loud.

I work every day to give wings to kindness
Encouraging all to do their best
I stand wincing against a wave of resistance
Waiting for indifference to crest.

With so many starving in the world
I feel their hunger pangs too
When you have laid crying alone in your bed
I've sat with you and cried with you too.

How did so many forget how to dream
Or to listen to their intuition
When did this great experience of life
Morph into one big institution.

Why did so many forget their purpose
Or how to manifest it into form
When did kindness, forgiveness, and truth
Become the exception instead of the norm.

I know when I became a wisp of myself
As silly as it may seem
We all lost sight of our humanity
The moment we forgot how to dream.

I Am Love

I am a Muslim
I declare my faith through kindness to all others.

I am a Jew
I have suffered dearly for my right to exist and have great resolve.

I am a Christian
I strive to personify Christ consciousness.

I am a Pagan
I see God in everyone and everything.

I am a Buddhist
I think and discern for myself.

I am an Atheist
I reject all tenets that do not resonate with my own sense of truth.

I am an Agnostic
I question everything, especially what others tell me to believe.

I am Gaia
I nurture all of life.

I am a Hindu
I believe in the continuity of life greater than this physical form.

I Am Love
I see the goodness in all others beyond all labels and personal convictions.

A Distant God

I'd like to meet most any God
That isn't based on love
Show him what he's doing to Earth
As push has come to shove.

He must have turned his head away
When his message was set in cause
There's such an inconsistency
Between love and obeying his laws.

Maybe he had a vision
That was just misconstrued
To have a noble intention
In everything we do.

There might be a miscommunication
That has to be set straight
Any God with any merit
Preaches love alone, not hate.

Maybe it's the concept
That so many are steeped in sin
Virtue is not a conquest or war
But simply going quietly within.

It's not about seeing the faults of others
Or bringing them down to their knees
It's seeing love in everyone
Let them worship as they please.

God is one pure intention
All must realize
It is Man who has buried the truth
And covered it with lies.

Any God that is a God
That is instilled in the hearts of Man
Doesn't incite the world to violence
Love has another plan.

Teach responsibility
In everything you do
If you judge in the name of God
That transgression is on you.

I can't agree with any man
Who diminishes others for God
But for all those imperfectly trying
It's their sincerity I applaud.

There is also a huge lesson
Bookmarked just for me
I can't micromanage everyone
I must let them all just be.

If I have judgment
In what others are ensuing
Then I am doing exactly what
I accuse them all of doing.

If I question what others value
With a cynical maraud
I myself am worshiping
A very distant God.

Life's Monument

Silence is the scourge of earth
When power and selfish combine
It's all that people think they can do
To watch without losing their mind.

They lose their voice, they hold their tongue
Terrified they themselves will wield power
When will they initiate their empowerment
Instead of dreading the final hour.

Being polite and just walking away
Were conditioned in us for a reason
When arrogance wears the mighty crown
Speaking truth is a grand act of treason.

White skin is the power suit of the day
Donned with its moral outrage
Does God play a hand in judging the masses
Or does truth speak through the healer and sage.

We all fear that trembling cadence of truth
When it finally shakes through the land
But does not always come as a volcanic eruption
It is revealed in each grain of sand.

The more we practice truth in our life
And challenge factions with, 'Why?'
The more we can crumble the spine of the bully
Causing both power and ignorance to die.

Why would God instill love in two hearts
And then somehow deem it as wrong
How come those who love seem so vulnerable
And those who hate seem so strong.

Why would God make us so different
Yet expect us to worship the same
Are people really so ignorant to believe
That they serve him when they kill in his name.

How does anyone gain our trust
Yet turn around and judge with such vengeance
Is there any room in someone's heart
To convert ignorance into transcendence.

Am I writing as an act of indulgence
Does anyone care about truth
Can someone change their stance in midlife
Or must we rely again on the youth.

Is anyone out there ready to agree
That they have always held power
Not to wield it against anyone
Or to redeem it in the final hour.

You are the God force contained in a body
Love is the prevailing cement
Truth is your bite, joy is your teeth
Your integrity is life's monument.

Buying Freedom

A thousand lives are currency
That convert to a moment of clarity
The pain and frustration we so quickly spend
Is the price of admission for the right to transcend.

The disdain that is forged in harboring a lie
Is the apathy accrued when we don't even try
The secrets we cling to in our darkest of hour
Constrict us from accessing our personal power.

The boundary lines between us and the night
Are where the wings of our freedom take flight
The heights that we attempt to arrive at by foot
Can be reached with one loving intention or look.

A dream that jolts us awake and aware
Can wipe out the onslaught of an ominous despair
A murmur becomes an echo and then a decree
When the seeker utters to themselves, 'I am free!'

The Example

The child who is given
Such little regard
Keeps to herself
Tries real hard.

That researches life
Through every exchange
Cries to herself
Loves through disdain.

The child who is taken
Less seriously
Gives of herself
So creatively.

The child who is never
Given a second glance
A second helping
Or even a chance.

The child who survives
By flying under everyone's sight
Who has make-believe friends
Who cries through the night.

The child who grows weary
Of feeling the pain
Loves every little creature
To keep from going insane.

This child should grow
Into a crotchety old coot
It's not that far-fetched
The point isn't moot.

But somewhere, somehow
Love intervened
To keep this child safe
From being completely demeaned.

This child is adopted
By nothing but grace
Though pain and its cousins
May show on her face.

This child grows to adulthood
Ahead of the curve
To the chagrin of abusers
Who think she has nerve.

Who does this child
Think that they are
To remain so intact
Smiling through every scar.

This child knew the suffering
Her small body could take
Was best felt in her
Rather than watch someone else ache.

The child took the suffering
And passed it right through
It was as if it was a mission
She needed to do.

This child is a survivor
Showing all that can see
That the plight of all others
Lives in you and in me.

So, take this child's example
Of how to pass pain
As a wisp of smoke leaving
And never a stain.

It doesn't matter if your life
Doesn't look like a success
Just continue to continue
And know you are blessed.

For every challenge you meet
That doesn't sweep you away
Just take a deep breath
And call it a day.

What Needs to Happen to Have Peace

Angels need a rest
Visions need to clear
Divides must be mended
All engagements must be fair.

Dust needs to settle
From the antics of all men
Gardens need to be replanted
We must return to Zen.

Wars must be unwaged
Fevers need to break
The proud and indignant
Must admit to their mistake.

Women must be valued
In every sect, shape, and kind
New perceptions must be given
To the deaf, mute, ignorant, and blind.

Truths must be spoken
All lies must then rescind
Illusion must be stripped away
Dissolved into the wind.

Innocence must be nurtured
Sheltered from guile and deceit
Homage paid to individuality
And laid against its feet.

An awakening from all slumber
That has rusted all resolve
An opening of love's floodgate
Anguish coaxed to dissolve.

Forgo all petty squabbles
In all we think, feel, say, and do
Then peace will rest upon the land
And settle itself in you.

Love's Beautiful Array

Hazel blue
Amber gray
It's only pigment
Anyway.

Cinnamon brown
Or almond skin
They're not tinctures
On the love within.

Either ruby lips
Or pale brown
Love's sweet kiss
In both resounds.

Flaccid skin
Or pulled real tight
It's merely a camouflage
Of love's inner light.

New Agers
Or conservative in thought
Merely live the love
As they are taught.

Why can't all stop
To realize
Love has no color
Age or size.

It has no preference
There is no sin
We all look the same
From within.

We all think the same
From our heart
There's no different vantage points
Driving us apart.

When someone is different
It is an opportunity to see
Love's beautiful array
In the universal We.

Getting to the Heart of It

I am the Muslim
I am the Jew
I am the old lady
Who lives in a shoe.

I am the matador
I am his cape
The targeted bull
At the back of his nape.

I am the frenzy
I am the calm
I am the corruption
I am its balm.

I am the eagle's
Discerning keen eye
I am the lawyer
With his quick-witted lie.

I am anywhere
Push comes to shove
I am below
As I am above.

I am every vantage point
That helps one to grow
I am the heat wave
I am the snow.

Anything the human
Heart can endure
I am the infection
I am the cure.

I am every experience
One needs to surmount
You can knock someone down
But don't count them out.

You can rob them of pride
And cause them to fall
Or shrivel them up
In an energetic ball.

But soon we'll all awaken
From this illusion and see
That we're all joyful and whole
Abundant, loving, and free.

Give a Life Its Due

When does life begin
Who am I to say
Who and what's important
To put it another way.

To defend the human zygote
Protect it to extremes
But ignore the plight of children everywhere
Is hypocrisy it seems.

How about quality of life
As people get up in arms
But when a precious child is born
Who ensures that it doesn't starve?

What if it's born a different race or creed
Or from a different land
Is it treated with the same regard
That a generic fetus can command?

Why does it seem so much better
To be born with skin that's white
Does this genetic propensity
Better assist a world in plight?

These are the questions I struggle with
In an unsettled part of me
How can one even claim to love God
Yet happily cut down a tree?

Why do so many still hate and judge
And think that it's okay
To subjugate those who are different
On behalf of the God of the day?

Why are guns so prevalent?
Why is it a sacred right to shoot?
Yet when one speaks of the right to not be shot
The point is dismissed as moot.

Why do my sincere questions
Fall on such deaf ears?
Why are so many indignant about God
While their actions say they don't care?

I've accumulated questions
From current events through the years
Like, how do you convert the closing of the Dow
Into human tears?

I will continue to ask the questions
Not caring what others may think
Maybe it'll help someone somehow
By committing these musings to ink

There's a reason why so many are scared
To let their views be heard
The infinite hypocrisies of Man
Is literally absurd.

Yet, if the quality of a single life
Can benefit from my point of view
Then I will happily do what I can
To give that life its due.

Bonded in Purpose

I am the sinner
I am the saint
I am the canvas
I am the paint.

I am the rocket
Also its spire
I am the tinder
I am the fire.

I am every experience
There possibly could be
I am the forest
I am each tree.

I am all secrets
Carried upon the wind
I ride each new wave
As I watch it rescind.

I am the echo
The tremble of each leaf
I exemplify each truth
Emotion, belief.

I get inside you
You get inside me
We are together
Exponentially.

We are the whisper
The reckoning of each truth
The salty old wise one
The arrogance of youth.

We crack our pods open
In this seedbed of life
We blurt out each wonder
We lament every strife.

We are the collective
Coming to a head
The young virgin bride
Being led to her bed.

We'll awaken disheveled
With new knowing eyes
Truth will be naked
To our glorious surprise.

We'll know the Id
Of our lonely desires
Was a prompting to greet
What now transpires.

The introduction of love
In an expansive new way
We are now bonded in purpose
In the dawn of each day.

Silent Majority

I hate in any way, shape, or form
When someone tells me what to be
It even makes me angry
To think that I'm not free.

There are so many people
Who like to tell me I am wrong
But others who appreciate truth
Remark that I am strong.

It feels like there are still some groups
That care what I believe
It's like they try to micromanage God
And how love is received.

There are seven billion ways on earth
To worship and to pray
As many as that even seems
That number's growing every day.

It doesn't really matter
What others expect of you
After all is said and done
It's your business what you do.

So, mute the judgment in your mind
Of what you think, say, be, or feel
It's your inner voice that needs tending
It's the only one that's real.

Take a leap of freedom
For yourself and all mankind
Step outside your comfort zone
Let your own voice rule your mind.

Advocate for animals
Speak openly to trees
Put your reputation out there
For whales, the needy, and bees.

There is a silent majority
That's gone deaf, dumb, blind, and mute
They cringe and they recoil
At any thought of dispute.

Yet the world has been uplifted
Flames of war must quickly die
Every soul must reclaim its wings
And remember how to fly.

Love's Best Lesson

I gave away my power one day
It was easy I confess
Someone smiled sweetly
Then I was possessed.

I have been stripped bare to the bones
Just like so many more
That in their desperate need to love
Became an open door.

We all were plundered, soiled, and spurned
Mangled, broken, and deprived
But with our great ability to love
Managed to survive.

Now's the time to make things whole
Through collecting all our parts
With dignity and grace intact
We repair all broken hearts.

By knowing when we take from others
We are stealing our own grace
Everyone else is merely us
Reflected in another face.

And when we give too easily
We weaken the collective all
Yet when we help another
We are answering our own call.

We have learned love's best lesson
When we finally believe
That to give the most to the All
We must graciously receive.

Your Average Best Friend

Very independent
Yet doesn't like to be alone
Loves a big family
Just not her own.

Enjoys the beach
But doesn't like to swim
Loves to compete
It is important that they win.

Loves every holiday
Is comfortable in a crowd
Every thought she thinks
Is verbalized out loud.

Prefers diner food
To five-star cuisine
Tries every diet
In women's magazine.

Never outclassed
Always in style
She's a signature martini
Topped off with a smile.

Speaking for the Unborn

I am a baby
Born into a hell
It was my life to forgo
Not a politician's to sell.

I am a child
Living a lie
That all you need is to be born
And happiness will comply.

I am a teenager
Struggling to fit in
There is so much pressure on me
When everything is a sin.

I am an adult
Struggling to make my own way
It's like moving through molasses
For a mere dollar a day.

I am the victor
Who survived at all cost
With no social empathy
When all hope was lost.

I am the voice of reason
Speaking for the unborn
Don't force them into families
Impoverished and forlorn.

Let them easily pass through
The membrane of quick sorrow
May they firmly re-land
In the hope of the morrow.

The Tiny Fleet of Sandy Hook Angels

A tiny fleet of angels
Graced the world one day
Seven years they walked the earth
Immersed in children's play.

We thought we knew their purpose
To be nurtured and uplift
Each assigned a special family
With which to share their gifts.

Each child is like a song of God
A sacred celestial tone
But the music ended abruptly one day
God called his angels home.

Now the world feels cheated
Because of what transpired
How could death so cruelly take
What heaven has inspired?

The world has gone complacent
Indifferent to the core
With this devastating wake-up call
The golden rule can be restored.

God in his infinite wisdom
Set sights on something grand
To restore the milk of human kindness
In the brotherhood of Man.

These children are etched in our hearts
On a canvas made of pain
Yet, where the scratch marks of anguish are carved
Their innocence remains.

This tiny fleet of angels
That reawakened the heart of Man
Is the golden instrument to mark and gauge
Where peace on Earth began.

The Sledgehammer

Mirages of strangers
Where family pride would swell
A husk of a house
Where a home should dwell.

Eating discouragement
Three square meals a day
Living in squalor
Is the family way.

Keeping one eye open
Where dreams should be
Reuniting with enemies
In sibling rivalry.

Fighting for scraps
Of your own peace of mind
Debasement and ridicule
A swift kick in the behind.

Loving your neighbor
With none for yourself
Keeping what's sacred
Locked away on a shelf.

This defeat is fertile soil
For self-discovery to grow
You are the seed
Life forces you to sow.

Emerging beyond all measure
Better than the best
You can finally awaken
Knowing it's all been a test.

Everything that's been thrown at you
Right from the start
Was merely a sledgehammer
To open your heart.

Beautiful Androgyny

Beautifully androgynous
Why should you have to choose?
To deny part of yourself
It's only yourself that you lose.

Intrinsically blended
Both female and the male
What intrigue in your dance of self
What depth you entail.

Beauty and strength
Blended all together
You've proven yourself
In all kinds of weather.

Why can't the whole world
Be as wonderful as you
Expressive, creative
Loving and true.

To Finally Expound

When did good men turn
To darkness from the light?
Perhaps when they ignored
The weak and vulnerable's plight.

When they hoarded good intentions
All but for themselves
Put the dreams of the collective
On some forgotten shelf.

Or, when they heard the anguished cries
That were sent upon the wind
Shrugged off a seeming chill in the air
Wrapped tighter in their chagrin.

Lapped up all the victories
And accolades as their own
Refuted simple truth
They were repeatedly shown.

Denied that little children
Were being put into the ground
Cracked their moral compass
With no means to rebound.

Growing on vines
Of ill will and despair
Devoid of all fruit
Or blossoms to share.

How do we coexist
With such malevolent intentions?
This world is in need
Of divinity's intervention.

Let's purge the world with our love
Singe the hate to the ground
Enable humanity
To finally expound.

CHAPTER 3

Nature

THE NATURAL WORLD is in constant and perfect balance with the ebb and flow of energy within the universe. It takes in and absorbs energy in one form, uses it for its own purpose, and then gives back energy in another form so that the broader ecosystem of all things can survive and thrive.

I am often awestruck by the harmony and balance of all living things and matter within the universe. As a trained scientist and engineer, I think about complex systems, the interconnection between various components within the system, and the feedback loops that keep the system in balance. It is almost like the natural world is the perfect complex system.

I sometimes wonder how this perfect complex system evolved. Was it by intelligent design, or was it because of some natural evolutionary process? When I talk to Jen about these lofty questions, both she and I tend to gravitate towards the latter as being the most likely.

There is something fundamental within the 'DNA' of the universe that drives it to evolve and expand in consciousness. This DNA is often loosely described as sacred geometry. Sacred geometric patterns exist all around us. They are the perfect shapes and patterns that form the fundamental templates for life in the universe.

One form of sacred geometry is the Fibonacci sequence and the associated Fibonacci spiral. The Fibonacci sequence is the series of numbers 0,1,1,2,3,5,8,13,21, etc. The next number in the sequence is formed by adding together the previous two numbers in the sequence. Simple right? The Fibonacci spiral is constructed by plotting the Fibonacci series on a grid. It looks like the diagram below.

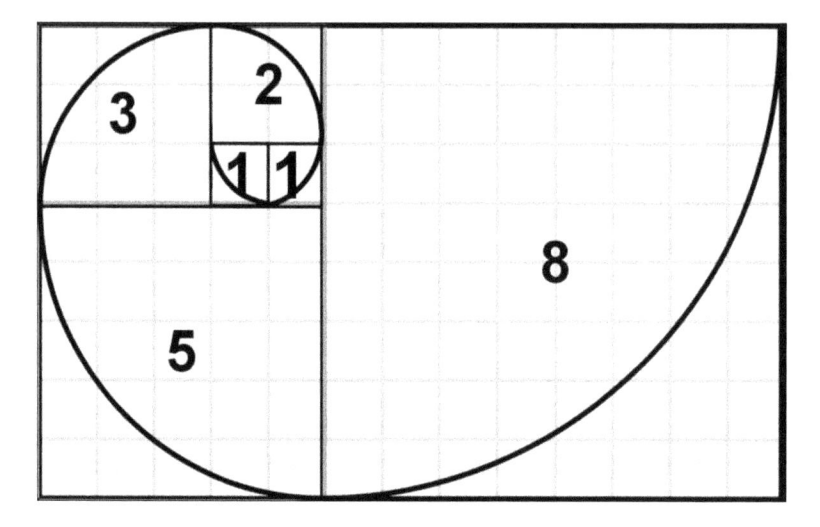

It turns out that the Fibonacci spiral is prevalent in nature. It is like it is the base code of universal structure and life itself. Examples of the Fibonacci spiral in nature are shown in the collage of images below.

Jenuine Poetry for Life | 71

Why is this important? Well, it shows that there is an underlying order within nature. All of nature is based on outflowing and expansion. It is intricately interconnected and balanced in the dance of energy. All animals perceive in energy as part of their sixth sense. Trees are connected to each other in energy through their root system. Birds collect and disperse stagnant energy as they fly.

So, it is interesting to note that humans are the one species on Earth that seem to be doing everything possible to control, harness, influence and subjugate the balance and harmony that is the natural state of being within the natural world.

Technology has allowed the human population to expand at an alarming rate. The extraction of fossil fuels and minerals has allowed us to produce all manner of goods and services for the excessive consumption pleasure of billions of people on the planet. But at what cost? All the pain, burden, limitations, disease, regret, and anxiety that people experience in the modern age is in large part the byproduct of being out of sync with nature.

And it gets worse. There are several people who are actively seeking to even further separate humanity from its natural environment by means of artificial intelligence. They promote the idea of dispensing with biological human systems altogether and propagating human consciousness throughout the universe in the form of self-replicating machines. Say what again?

I remember Jen describing in excruciating detail the anguish she experienced when reliving an engram of her consciousness being trapped in a cyborg body. She describes it as the loneliest experience possible. And she says that many people welcome pain in their present life because it is much better than the hollowness of having your consciousness eternally trapped in a cyborg body that has no feeling at all.

Our destiny is not to propagate human consciousness throughout the universe by means of machines and artificial intelligence. It is to expand in consciousness and to transcend the ego to the point where the soul can finally penetrate the membrane of the etheric plane and therefore to exist within the higher worlds.

Jen often recalls that some people in her private sessions are terrified of transcending the ego because they think that in doing so, they will be disconnected from their consciousness and identity. They think that existing in the higher worlds is like an existence of nothingness. We both feel that this is a misconstruction.

All that exists in the universe is programmed to outflow and expand in consciousness. Beings that exist in the higher worlds may no longer require a physical body. But that doesn't mean they exist in a state of nothingness. They outflow and expand universal consciousness through their interaction and guidance of beings in the lower worlds to assist them in their journey towards transcendence. I suspect this is an apt description of what the Adepts are doing as part of their purpose. Jen often says that souls that have transcended the ego are able to easily traverse between the higher worlds and the lower worlds. They do from time to time take physical form in the lower worlds for a specific purpose.

I think it is vitally important that we disrupt the programming of those seeking to take humanity down a path of machine based artificial intelligence. One of the best ways to do this is for all of us to reconnect with nature, and to rejoin the natural evolution of souls in the natural world. Putting the effort into learning to communicate with nature is a great way to accelerate your ability to tap into your own divinity.

Jen in an avid nature communicator. I remember laughing myself silly in the early days of our interaction when I read on her LinkedIn profile that her additional languages are Dog, Cat, Fish and Tree!

Jen and I have run several three-hour workshops to help people communicate with trees as part of a process to enhance their abilities to perceive in energy, tap into direct knowingness, and access higher consciousness. In those workshops, Jen provided practical advice on how to interact and communicate with trees, including the following:

- Sit under a tree and ask to see the world from its vantage point.
- Read to a tree so that it can see the world from your vantage point.
- Blowing on a tree is a way to kiss it in its own language.
- A tree can bond with you through your touch. If you give it some of your spittle, it can read your energy to know what your needs are.
- Peeing under a tree is an intimate way of sharing with it (not suggested in public parks).
- Trees love to be sung to, so sing to your favorite tree. They will in turn inspire you to write your own songs. Many of the great song writers were downloading what the trees were giving them.
- Have a conversation with a tree like it is your best friend.
- Water a tree's bark and see if it pulls the clouds in for a rain shower.
- When trees drop limbs or fruit, they are trying to get your attention. They do this to connect with you.
- Trees say thank you through a rustling of the wind.
- Trees don't like nails or metal in them of any kind. It is compassionate to remove them.
- Clean up the trunk and surrounds of a tree. Trees love to know they are cared for.
- Trees love to be validated. To listen to a tree is a way to get them to speak more with you. The more you listen, the more they will give you.

- Trees will never admonish you in a harsh way. They may give a little bit of tough love if you climb them or pick fruit off them without permission.
- Trees can tell you things that it knows from its history. The older a tree is, the longer its resume of information that it can share with you.
- If you want to get into a creative moment, do the project under your tree and ask for its help.

Of course, trees are not the only form of nature that you can reconnect with. Jen actively speaks to all forms of nature, both animate and inanimate. That is why she is so connected with her plushies.

The poems and artwork that follow in this chapter explore various aspects of nature. May they inspire you to reconnect with nature as part of your own spiritual journey.

Marvin Schneider
Wodonga, Australia
March 2022

Homage to the Foliage

Hear the tiny million voices
From all the world around
Feel the little advocates
And the blessings that abound.

Perceive their angst
And plight to thrive
Know their calling
I AM ALIVE.

Perceive them crying
To be seen
I am not human
But I am green.

Sense them linger
In your heart
We are not separate
We do our part.

Acknowledge their gift
Show them you care
We are your breath
We make your air.

We make life pretty
We heal your stress
When you're with us
You worry less.

We buffer sounds
That are too harsh
We bring the stillness
Of the marsh.

We help all people
Quietly refrain
From collectively
Going insane.

So, thank your flowers
Your grass, a tree
They make us all
A better Me.

Sighting

The concave line on an inner circle
Parallel to the setting sun
Framed by the arch of myth or legend
An oblique sighting of what could have been won.

The brightest star in the farthest dimension
Waving whimsical and free
Was it in a dream or aspiration
That I recognize that star as me?

Mortar and Sticks

As we tend the livestock
Let's work hand in hand
On the spiritual acreage
Of our own wonderland.

Fertilizing the orchards
Shearing the sheep
Intentions are the promises
We are committed to keep.

We'll teach the world's businessmen
A noble pursuit
Service to community
As they harvest the fruit.

Instilling in them
The golden rule
Those serving with integrity
Are nobody's fool.

You tend the bread kitchen
I'll nurture baby chicks
We build a new reality
With dreams, mortar, and sticks.

We'll lay down the foundation
In energy and in deed
Everyone is accountable
In producing the mead.

Graciousness and surrender
Go hand in hand
May we expound all of humanity
Simply by loving the land.

GMOs

Hell No! I won't go
Don't turn me into a GMO.

All this worry just tears me apart
I want to keep my human heart.

Please don't make my skin out of rubber
I'd cry saline tears when I blubber.

Please don't give me silicon eyes
That are kept in boxes in medical supplies.

First it was veggies, now it is trees
Soon they'll be making mechanical bees.

I don't want to evolve into a drone
I want progress and science to leave me alone.

The world should be left organic and green
I echo the cries of voices unseen.

Every living organism wants to remain real
Think of the inhumanity, how would you feel?

If all of your gifts, your intangible wealth
Was removed so you'd last longer on a shelf.

If our essence, our nature was stripped clear away
So we'd look better when we were put on display.

Everything we do to others could happen to us
If those who know better don't put up a fuss.

It's against our nature to have to disagree
But for humanity's sake we must make this plea.

Stop this human arrogance that thinks only of self
Or someday it will be humans who are kept on a shelf.

H_2O

We curse the water for pouring down
We blame it all for freezing
We curse it when it floods the ground
We curse it every season.

We blame it when it collects in clouds
When its downpours steal our thunder
We poison it with toxic waste
And rob it of its wonder.

We pour crude sugar in each glass
To make it much more tasteful
We desecrate its purity
Abuse it and are wasteful.

Taking for granted what is vital to us
May be part of our decline
Others can dis what's 75% of them
I will be grateful for mine.

More than Family

Listen close
And you will hear
Constant reassurance
A sympathetic ear.

A lick of the face
In agreement I suppose
The surprising delight
In an ice-cold nose.

The wag of a tail
The warm spot in your bed
The unbridled acceptance
From that tail to the head.

Toenails that tap
As paws scamper on the floor
They are not here to obey
They are here to adore.

They are closer than family
We chose them from the start
They are more than a friend
They are an extension of our heart.

Any Day

Any new day is a sacred occasion
Any ole day is a benchmark to mark
Any new day is the first day of summer
Any day is a new dog's first day in the park.

Any day is a day to give thanks and worship
A labyrinth, adventure, new season or birth
Any day is a great one to behold and to treasure
Any day is the best one to be here on earth.

Any day is the dawn of a clear new perspective
Glorious, exhilarating, reverent and new
Any day is how I want to spend my forever
Any day is every day when I spend it with you.

The Moment

The quivering line between horizon and ocean
The magnetic play between stillness and motion.

The oil of the sweat of a labor of love
The knee jerk relief when escaping a shove.

Ten million moments conjoined in an hour
The disarming grace of a play without power.

The biting cry of a fallen bird's call
Recovering your dignity after a fall.

The rhythm created while writing a poem
The sanctity felt when journeying home.

Gaia Speaks

The cold strikes the human sky
Huddled in dwellings the settlers ask, 'Why?'
Buried in arrogance and piles of snow
Believing there's nothing they don't already know.

As a species they desecrate all natural gifts
Indifference accumulates in heavy white drifts
Cycles of weather come, and they go
Indolence the only fruit Man's willing to sow.

So many lessons left on the table
Humanity crippled by the willing and able
Power let out one last haughty laugh
Willing to sacrifice the last fatted calf.

It will run this world to the ground
Frack it to ashes, a lifeless mound
Until Gaia stepped in with an even brow
To balance the scales in the here and now.

Dispensing truth that was once called treason
Gifting many with the ability to reason
Restoring justice back to the land
As a handful stand by who can understand.

There's no need to hoard what's in the ground
When abundance and blessings are all around
There's no need to take an eye for an eye
You can hear the plea in Goddess' cry.

Abundance for all, the original decree
Is restored to every man, animal, species, and tree
Taking for taking's sake is finally disarmed
Greed, glitz, and gluttony stripped of its charm.

Abuse of power has become the enemy at large
As it finally sinks in, man's no longer in charge
In this ruthless weather, one stark truth ensues
The restoration of humanity is an expression of you.

Thinking you are unworthy, unable to cope
Is telling everyone to give up all hope
Get off your ass, shake off the crumbs
Pound feeling back into your limbs that went numb.

You're not on the sidelines of some spectator sport
You are here to get messy, get involved, give support
Thinking false humility is good is part of the lie
You can see through the illusion if you give it a try.

Everyone is a superhero with their own special power
Your gifts are your wine, don't stagnate and sour
Embrace what makes you special, it is truly your gift
The weather will break, the clouds will all lift.

One more truth that you really need to believe
Gaia speaks to your heart as you learn to receive.

One and the Same

Miles of stroked silk
Each sheath touched with dew
Braised by the elements
Soaked in emerald hue.

Turquoise skies
With clouds for lace
Smile down sweetly
On this holiest place.

Bloodstained soil
Hide the white man's sin
Echoes in soft whispers
Are carried on the wind.

The Elder's timeless pleas
To their forefathers above
Are finally redeemed
Through nature's purging love.

Massive ancient graves
Beholding reverent names
Purge the sacred soils
Of humanity's foolish games.

The indigenous rise up
To reinstate their ancient claim
That peace and love of the land
Are one and the same.

CHAPTER 4

Ascension

I HAVE PREVIOUSLY touched on the idea that the purpose of life is to outflow and expand universal consciousness through your experiences in a series of incarnated lives within the lower worlds. I have also touched on the drive to transcend the ego as an opportunity to slip through the membrane of the etheric plane and therefore gain access to the higher worlds.

What we are really talking about here is the process of ascension. Ascension is another word for enlightenment, the achievement of which is a primary objective for many people within the spiritual community.

I am aware that some spiritual paths adopt the idea that enlightenment is the holy grail, which once attained puts you at the lofty heights of gurus, saints, and siddhas. It is certainly the case that ascended masters are to be treasured. This is because they tend to take on the role of a spiritual teacher.

But as Jen describes it, the traditional 'guru' image of ascended masters is no longer relevant. More and more ascended masters are living and operating in the 'real' world, in local communities, and in plain sight. And while they are enlightened, they still face real (if not unique) challenges in living and operating within the harsh vibration of the lower worlds. Jen is one example of this. I will describe Jen's journey to ascension later in this chapter introduction.

Earth and humanity are at a tipping point. There is a real risk that the Earth can be destroyed, and the human experiment come to an end, if a critical mass of humans do not ascend now. This is why there are so many spiritual teachers, spirit guides, advanced beings, and Adepts working tirelessly with humanity to assist in this mass ascension process. They are all doing their part. So, it would behoove us all to pay attention and do the work required for our own ascension.

Mainstream religion and societal norms teach us to be good. But in a lot of ways, focusing on being good denies us the opportunity to recognize the aspects of ourselves that are not good. Part of the purpose of life as a spiritual being having a human experience is to have ALL experiences of duality within your repertoire – both positive and negative. Old souls[4] will have had many thousands of incarnated lives within the lower worlds. In more than a few of them, you will have been both the perpetrator and the victim of truly horrible scenarios. So, none of us are as pure as the driven snow.

Enlightenment is a formulaic process. It is all about looking at yourself in totality. In the process of ascension, you will be pushed to the brink of insanity to recognize your own dark nature, and when pushing through it, you will realize that it is all an illusion. You will then enjoy three days of bliss in an egoless state. At the end of those three days, the ego rejoins the soul because the ego is required to survive within the lower worlds. But from that time on, the

---

[4] There is a debate within the spiritual community as to whether all people on Earth now are old souls. Jen is inclined towards the idea that we are all old souls who have had the necessary experiences to begin the ascension process.

soul is always keeping the ego in check to make sure it does not run amok again.

As Jen describes it, ascended masters have sufficient awareness and connection to the macrocosm that they are no longer driven to reincarnate habitually. They have had all the experiences they need to accumulate in the lower worlds, and they have transcended the ego. However, it seems that many ascended masters choose to reincarnate into the lower worlds for the purpose of assisting humanity in the mass ascension process. Others it seems, outflow and assist humanity in an energy body and not in a corporeal form.

I have heard it said that going through the process of enlightenment requires being pushed to the edge of insanity. That is certainly true in Jen's case.

She had left her ordinary life to move in with a sociopath in a state in America which was home to neither of them. They weren't romantically involved. But because of her lack of intimate relationships and feelings of unworthiness, she agreed to be with someone who was obsessed with aliens, well versed on alternate realities, and psychically acute.

Jen was suddenly isolated from all she knew. She was sensory deprived from restrictions he put on her. She was able to access all his insanity as if it were her own. On top of that, he went from being kind to her, to accusing her of stealing his abilities. He became paranoid of her and started accusing her of being the enemy.

She was alienated even more by being told she was the cause of all the suffering in the world. A lot of negative personas were accredited to her, like Darth Vader, Jack the Ripper, and even the devil. She was constantly berated, sleep deprived, and constantly reminded of how bad she was.

She was forced to drink glass after glass of vinegar water to flush out the negativity in her. She was also forced to take high doses of niacin which caused a violent reaction in her body, turning it beet red with excruciating hives and leathery skin. In this state, the sociopath would make her look in the mirror and see herself as Satan himself.

Her sense of self became drastically skewed. When she closed her eyes, she would see horrific imagery from the viewpoint of depravity. A common one was being an old man chained to a wall amongst a million other prison cells. He was emaciated and naked except for a rotted loincloth. There was a hole in the rugged rock wall that poured a paste of sewage into his reach. His only means of sustenance was to eat it. The world above him was clueless or indifferent to the misery of millions like him.

A few scenarios of a depravity would play through Jen's mind that pushed her to the edge of insanity. For example, an evil genius created lab specimens to generate energy. One was a biologically generated rat that was a living ball of many rats combined in one. It had many legs and many heads, each of which was trying to run in its own direction. This inner conflict was a means to collect energy to be fed on. The same laboratory kept an innocent little girl perched alone in a dark cage. This was another means of feeding off the goodness of others.

There were regular scenarios of debauchery that repeated themselves at quicker intervals. There was a weird burlesque show with one man wearing only a boa entertaining in a club by stimulating himself as he danced and ejaculating on the audience. There were horrific monsters of the 1950's horror flicks entering a dungeon room with a beautiful woman and ravaging her in rape. There was a cave where creations of a mad genius existed.

Within all the ugly imagery were the first drawings of Disney characters in their rudimentary form. They were eerily frightening in their contrast with the other scenes. They were just another means of feeding on people's energy through drawings of cute sympathetic characters. She would see the formulation of their early drawings dancing in a lab. She didn't understand the significance of this until much later. It was using the innocence of people to draw them into willingly giving up their energy to their own demise. The world is being destroyed by big business. Yet people continue to agree with their existence to feed some small creature comfort. It is like their imagination itself is being harvested and distorted and used to control humanity.

The neighbors, who the sociopath thought were members of the illuminati, seemed to take a special interest in Jen. They would only show up when Jen was pushed to the wall and trying to leave. Then there was a grandmotherly woman who started inviting them over for picnics. The head of house would come over when Jen wasn't working hard enough and encourage the sociopath to work her harder.

She cleared a lot of brush, stumps and trees in the hundred-degree Fahrenheit heat to seemingly extract the last bit of stamina from her. All the brush that she cleared out from acres of land was collected into a huge brush pile that was bigger than two or three houses next to each other. This pile stayed in the back yard until the neighbors felt it was safe to burn it.

The night Jen went through enlightenment was maddening for her. The sociopath was telling her that she was the evil in the world that needed to be destroyed. She and he went from saving the world together, to her being the one that they were saving the world from. This set her mind in a loop of denial, justification and finally succumbing to this reality. It pushed her through the 'eye of the needle.'

When she looked at the wall, the shadowy images of debauchery became more and more alive. They started to dance on the wall and pull her in. She was drawn at warped speed through a tunnel of different experiences. For her, it felt like going through rooms at an alarming speed with a thin sheet separating each room from the last. It was her zooming through all of her lifetimes at warped speed and landing in a new realm.

The cave she got used to visiting in her dreams was now gutted of all its debauchery. It was an empty cavern where the sun now pierced through. Everything was cleansed by the light. The mad scientist's laboratory was gone. All the inventions and creations of a selfish mind were gone. Even the prison cell containing the old man in the loin cloth was empty and the door was open. She was walking in a clean cavern.

She was drawn outside to overlook a beautiful world. The cave always seemed like it was underground. But now it was at a high altitude overlooking the world. She observed a courtyard below. There was the Disney princess Cinderella and her prince dancing in a beautiful spring scenery. The seasons changed right before her eyes as they danced. She was being shown an understanding beyond time. She was controlling the change of seasons with her mind.

Her attention was drawn to the sky. There was a planet being formed like a soap bubble being formed through a wand. Then there was another, and another, and another. She then knew that she was creating these planets with her imagination and her intentions. She wondered whether they would be peaceful and loving planets or ones of war and discord. This was her being taught the ramifications of her thoughts and responsibility to always create planets of substance and integrity with her intentions.

Then she was pulled back into the body with alarming speed. In the corner of the room was a huge tubular membrane from ceiling to floor that took up a huge section of the room. It emitted a sickening rhythmic sound that was the antithesis of joy. It sounded a lot like the chant of the scary monkeys in the Wizard of Oz movie. It was a throbbing pulsing rhythmic vortex of power. It was difficult for her to be so close to it. She was physically nauseous and disoriented.

She continued to lay in place and try to orient herself. But if she opened her eyes, a shadow appeared on the wall of an orgy scene. First it was an outline like hand shadows. Then it started to dance in place and became filled with detail. As soon as she focused on it, she was pulled out of her body from within and taken on another excursion. This kept happening as she tried to stay present in her body. She kept being sucked out of her body through the dancing image of the orgy on the wall.

She started to cry. She admitted to the sociopath how awful she was and all the things she had done and all the imagery she was seeing. She was surprised when he had compassion for her and talked nicely to her. This helped her to relax. It was then that she realized she was different. All the jealousy and pettiness that was being triggered in her was gone. All the self-consciousness and scrutiny was gone. She was at peace. This was apparent to the sociopath as well. She got to sit up for the first time in days.

As nighttime fell, there was a validation that something had shifted. The huge pile of brush that she had collected since she arrived on the property was being lit on fire by the neighbor. It was a huge blaze in the night sky. It was somehow an exhilarating expansiveness of freedom. It was also a form of validation to Jen that this experience she was having was a collaboration and it was important to the world. At this stage, she had no great sense of her healing abilities or her contribution to humanity through her writings and SFT tapping protocols. But for some reason, her going through this experience was important in the greater scope of life.

For three days she was able to be outside. She experienced a purity of an egoless state. The sweet resolve and peace she felt were a contrast to the racing and strategizing of the average mind. She thought this peace was her new natural state. The sound abomination in the corner was fading. She could still be easily pulled out of her body through the imagination, but it became more controllable. Her senses were still very heightened and acute. But then she got a sense of an unsettling 'presence' returning to her.

She thought it was an evil overtaking her because of the coarseness of its vibration. But it was just the ego being returned to her. She was told inwardly that the ego is a necessary mechanism for protection while in the physical world. What we call enlightenment is the ego getting pulled out and cleansed while the physical, emotional, causal and mental bodies realign. Then the ego is returned to the body.

The ego assists us in staying present in the physical body and allows us to navigate the reality of the lower worlds while also being aware of the vastness of the universe we are actually a part of. The veil between this world and the others is monitored by the ego. It only allows information through that is deemed helpful to one's physical existence. All the striving and seeking up until the point of enlightenment is trying to convince the ego that truth is relevant to your physical life.

People think that enlightenment will give them a great advantage over others. But it took Jen a few more months to get out of the living situation that she was in. This egoless state that was now part of her makeup was described by the sociopath as being like a retarded boy.

It took Jen almost ten years to process this experience as being the process of enlightenment. And as dynamic as it might seem to the reader, it was simply Jen's own personal story of survival. Jen is convinced that everyone's own experience is much more satisfying than knowing of hers. But if it helps people tap into their own enlightenment, then she is happy to share.

Jen believes that she went through this horrific process so that others can access the experience of enlightenment without having to go through the terrifying experience alone. Perhaps all the insanity in the world is people all over the world being pulled through the process of enlightenment themselves and feeling terrified at the natural isolation of it.

Perhaps it will benefit others to understand that this experience of their own private hell has a purpose and a completion. Perhaps realizing that others are passing through it as well is important. Jen says ascension is a formulaic process of being forced to look at all of the aspects of humanity that reside within us, accepting them as an aspect of ourselves, and pushing past the illusion of their reality.

Enlightenment is an experience that all beings will eventually go through. When one person goes through it, it makes it easier for others to go through. Whereas in past times, the holy man would come down from the mountain to be worshipped, it's time now for all those who come down from the mountain to design the best blueprint as possible for others to pass through enlightenment. This is the key to mass enlightenment, and this is the intention we put into sharing all of Jen's writings.

The upgrade in the fifth dimension is the coming together of soul mates in service of humanity as two aspects of the same intention. I like to think that this is exactly what Jen and I are doing. It has been a long time coming. But our reconnecting has occurred at exactly the right time to assist all of humanity to ascend.

The poems and artwork that follow in this chapter explore various aspects of the ascension process. May they trigger within you the conditions to initiate your own ascension process.

Marvin Schneider
Wodonga, Australia
March 2022

Winning the Human Race

I love you through all eyes
Feel you through all skin
Hold you through all arms
Am happy when you win.

I cry when you are sad
Hurt when you feel pain
Shine on you like the moon
I wax and then I wane.

You have no real enemies
No reason for disgrace
You are loved beyond your station
You are loved beyond your race.

There's no need to be diminished
No reason to feel small
Living scared or helpless
Serves nobody at all.

We all began believing
We were separate and alone
And that we had these sins to bear
For which we must atone.

But love rushed through and washed away
The smallness that we hide
It broke through all defenses
To free the love inside.

It ignited every ember
Like the one inside of you
To exonerate all trespasses
And let that love pierce through.

See, it never was about
Walking aimlessly alone
It was experiencing every vantage point
Of which you thought you must atone.

It is learning true compassion
For every form of life
Sometimes as the husband
Sometimes as the wife.

Once you can truly know
What's going on with another
Then every different form of life
Truly is your brother.

And when that happens to us all
There's compassion for the rest
The heart of humanity will burst forth
We'll have passed the final test.

We all together will transcend
Walking hand in hand
Integrity and kindness
Will ring throughout the land.

Everything we've done so far
We will totally erase
We will finally stop the madness
And win the human race.

Transcendence

Beyond Godly borders
Upon which nationality depends
Is the universal war cry
For humanity to transcend.

All the etchings in marble
And the writings in stone
Are left to remind us
We don't do it alone.

Walls are not made
To keep us living in fear
Bridges are built
To spread truth everywhere.

Beyond the façade
Of what we all know
Is good versus evil
Going toe to toe.

The same struggle that takes place
Between us and our brethren
Is reflective of what's fought
Between our hell and our heaven.

The same battle that's fought
In our family and home
Is the same that played out
In ancient Athens and Rome.

The same selfish desires
And pettiness of plans
Is seen a billion times over
In the struggle of Man.

When we conquer our dreams
Put the ego in check
Take a moment from the drama
Take time to reflect.

It is clearly visible
That on which we depend
Is an illusion that evaporates
Once we transcend.

Every Angel

I gazed upon a feather
Just to know its charms
The down barbules waved rhythmically
Like tiny little arms.

They showed a flexibility
It's quill a quiet stance
From this new perspective
Began a new romance.

Once you truly see something
Take it in from all directions
It's nearly quite impossible
To not develop true affections.

This is a key to mastering life
A skill one can depend
Means to unfurl such beautiful wings
And finally to transcend.

If you can look at anyone
Beyond all pain and strife
Become enamored with their quiet virtue
Then you can love all life.

No longer will you be imprisoned
Grounded by the Id
You will become immortal
Just like every angel did.

Awakening

Within crusted walls of embedded emotion
Bombarded by waves of perpetual commotion
Is a permanent Me determined to stand
Slough off adversity like layers of sand.

Draw in the light from a faraway source
To stand firm in the love seems par for the course
Reverberating in music, a most precious choir
Break through the dross, confusion, and mire.

Emanate, vibrate, reverberate, resound
Inundated with such beauty, I unfurl and rebound
Showing others imprisoned what awakening can be
Humbly resonating beautiful and free.

The Awakened

Truth withdrew into the mist
As ignorance blew its one last kiss
Many receded with the tide
To wait for power to subside.

A few stood strong in soul's dark night
To help the wounded retake flight
They stood with backs against the wind
Waiting for the darkness to rescind.

Control is the boil on power's decree
Brokers and pawns vestige their one last plea
Fear, anger, jealousy is their stance
To manipulate who leads in the final dance.

Many awaken in the final round
Many more warriors start to rebound
Those that were fractured beyond compare
Spontaneously heal and start to repair.

The wind is mild, the current is right
For the multitudes to take flight
They pull away from power's last try
Join the legion of awakened into the sky.

Artistry

My life is the canvas
On which I paint my truth
Wisdom intervened for me
From spilling my paint in youth.

Inspiration is the well
In which I dip my pen
I'm commissioned by the gods
Yet judged in turn by men.

The canvas may crack and dry
The lessons long ferment
But the artist stands by her work
Not one stroke do I regret.

Living in Zen

Don't need to stay
Don't feel like going
Original ideas
Perpetually flowing.

No judgment here
No points to belabor
Every moment of peace
Is one to be savored.

Nothing to prove
No one to belittle
The world is aligned
By staying in the middle.

Each soul met
Is great amongst men
Honor their presence
By living in Zen.

Soul Trail Blazer

Cast a net upon the shore
Let it rest upon the surface
Draw it back with mindful regard
Of its duality of purpose.

Draw abundance to yourself
Let gratitude be its drag
Others churn in overt waters
Their curses are their plague.

Leave behind the gritty bitters
The natural backwash of the brew
Say grace over the elixir
Something others will fail to do.

Etch your name upon the table
Soft wood kept under glass
Leave a note for the next soul traveler
In a weatherworn sealed flask.

Incarnating

Incarnating is how angelic beings descend
A mosaic arrangement of when light and sound blend
A delicate instrument dancing in flesh
Joyous love mix with pain in a temporal mesh.

Their voice is the song of their limited decree
Of all they believe and to what they'll agree
Their eyes see through filters of limited light
Focused on what they believe to be right.

Their hands meld and transform ideals
In a limited lot
The painter, the healer
What's possible, what's not.

Ears carve out a ventral
Of limited scope
That puts less into knowing
And more into hope.

Their legs track the land
With the stubbornest of will
Only a relentless regard
Of what they wish to fulfill.

Until the whole process
Is put back into the ground
Soul agrees once again
To be physically bound.

That's What You Do

No one can touch your head
To make you feel sane
No one can talk you through
A whole life of disdain.

No one can see your whole forest
They'll fixate on one tree
Live your whole life for you
Or tell you how to be.

No one can broach
The depths that you reach
Not by virtue, devotion
Or flowery speech.

The path that you're on
You venture alone
So, make it count for something
Make it your own.

Take back all the power
You've strewn along the way
Collect it back up
You'll need it someday.

You are the only expert
On what it's like to be you
There's no one alive
Who can fit in your shoes.

Save your energy
For what lies ahead
As you forge your own way
Make your own bed.

The love that propels you
Comes from only one source
The universe itself
Has sanctioned your course.

So don't play it small
Or cower to the masses
They can't see your greatness
Not even with glasses.

You will fall through the cracks
Your sense of pain will be heightened
You will feel like a failure
Until you're enlightened.

The path then won't be easier
Not by afar
But at least you can watch it
Perched on a star.

Then you will see other souls
Try to shimmer as well
Overcome obstacles
Their own private hell.

Send them a lifeline
What else can you do
You love so very deeply
That's what you do.

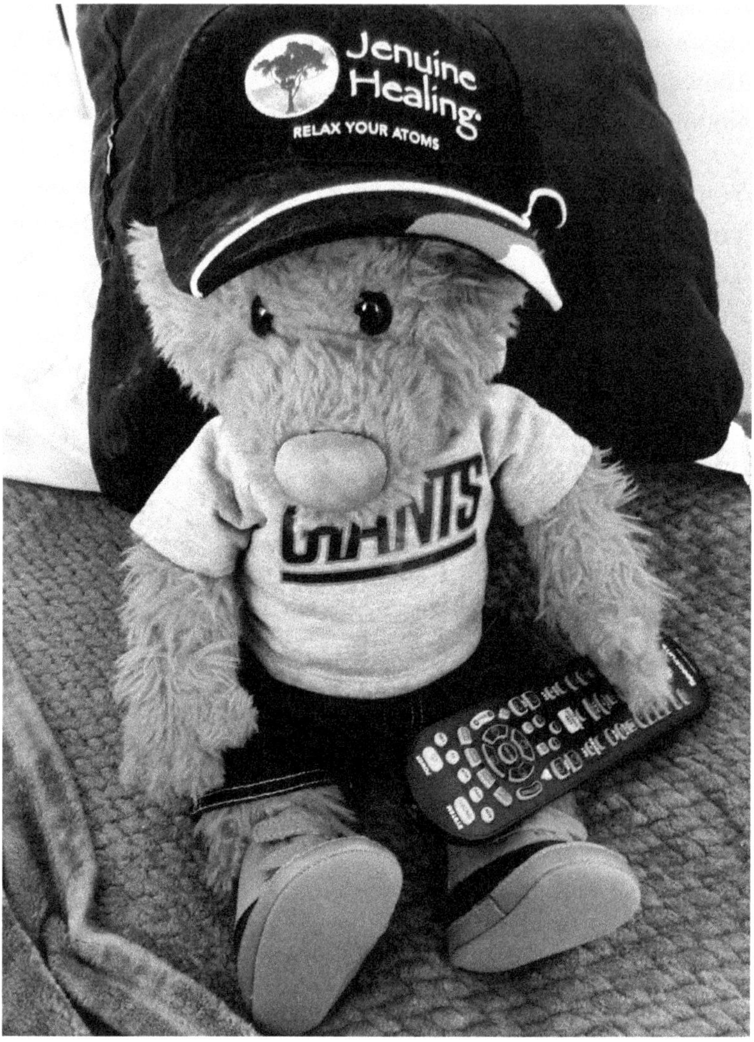
Jenuine
Healing
RELAX YOUR ATOMS

Omniscience

Toss your atoms into the air
Catch them on the wind
Scatter them beyond all reason
Where time and space begin.

Throw your voice into the sky
To worlds beyond the night
Follow it to that ageless place
Where your true self first took flight.

Twirl and revel in your joy
Dance partner with a star
Realize the personified love
That you really are.

A New Person

Being renewed each moment
To the one I am at the core
More free, lighter, and happier
Than a moment before.

I can sing my own praises
Dance in the mist or the rain
I can embrace every tragedy
It helps let go of the pain.

I can swim with the fishes
Although it is only in my mind
I talk with dolphins, whales, and seals
Leave all illusion behind.

I consult with my mentors
The ancient wisdom of trees
They whisper long standing truths
Sent to me on the breeze.

I can withstand almost anything
Loss, loneliness, the plight of our youth
But I can't bear the lies of this world
I'll no longer bury my truth.

Which is…

You are a mystery waiting to reveal
You are the answer you seek
Open yourself up and just look inside
Whatever you tell you, just speak.

Sing it to all who will listen
Knowing much will fall on deaf ears
But it is so worth the performance
If just one person can hear.

It's time to embrace the wisdom of The Trees

Self-Realization

Re-adjust your magnetic North
Circumnavigate your inner course
Wax and wane without a mention
Of loss, pain, or remorse.

Regroup from the ebb
Throw yourself back into the flow
Recycle all conception of loss
Get back to what you know.

Transcend the concepts of limitation
Gather all possibilities into the now
Beyond the inhale and exhale of hope's expectation
Embrace it with a simple WOW.

Mastery

Making a lefthand turn
Without help of a light
Gaining ownership
Over your second sight.

Thriving beyond
Any disease
Encouraging creativity
Let it do as it please.

Walking a tight wire
Without the use of a net
Living and loving
Without any regret.

Finding adventure
Behind every door
Being your best ever
Then ten percent more.

What It Is to Be Free

I am a cavern that love pours in
The echo of sound, crisp as the wind
Beckons me to quench thirst for truth
With the skill of a craftsman and eagerness of youth.

All my atoms are charged, I can do no wrong
They are eager and lithe, empowered, and strong
Pulled from the illusion of form
Just as the heat of the sun squelches the storm.

In an altered state, I experience I Am
If I can transcend, everyone can
My atoms that know that I am inevitably free
Stretch through the universe, greet all that is me.

While the mind thinks it's this solid matter
Your atoms are craving permission to scatter
To stretch through the universe as ambassadors of you
Overtake your denial with what's really true.

In this way, we all blend and blur
We discover the secret to how to endure
Knowing what we experience under ego's rule
Is our personal lesson plan in our own private school.

In energy we are never so trapped
We go wherever our imagination is wrapped
The only prison that there really can be
Is the mind that can't fathom what it is to be free.

Enlightenment

Open up the floodgates
Between the human and divine
Rest yourself in sweat-stained sheets
Let your ego lay supine.

Offer yourself up to the inner worlds
That beckon you to undress
The real self walks in brilliant wonders
That the mind cannot suppress.

Bring a gift back to this world
A memory or insight
Leave it as a bread crumb trail
So others may take flight.

How to Transcend

Be aware of your own actions
Experience your own worth
Accept the rejection
At the moment of your birth.

Stand by your convictions
Whatever they may bring
Delve into all your talents
To dance, act, write, or sing.

Marvel at the wonders
A banquet to mankind
Connect with others deep within
Way beyond the mind.

Live past the constrictions
Of what one can endure
Raise the bar on accountability
With motives that are pure.

Rake the shoals of society
To glean a spark in Man
Ignite a billowing fire
As only pure love can.

Lift humanity on your shoulders
Let it see that which you see
Beyond the walls of the self
All empowered, inspired, and free.

Encouragement of a Full Moon

Stand between the sun and moon
Let the love and light pass through
Illuminate your bountiful heart
Drop the extraneous part called You.

Magnify your bountiful heart
To the size and width of Earth
Treat it as a looking glass
To show others their ultimate worth.

Hold the reflection steadily
Ignore the negative onslaught
Love breezes clean every last atom
Before its true essence is caught.

Be unwavering as the moon and the sun
Match their luminescent light
Allow others to realize the brilliancy of truth
By accessing their own second sight.

Span across the globe of Man
Rise above the stagnant air
Pierce the earth with your magnified love
Let it feel the extent of your care.

Become one with the body of Earth
Let the sun and moon's light pass straight through
Expand the atoms to an omniscient state
Allow truth to align in you.

Be the surrogate of the highest purpose
In the humanity of Man
Yes, it's possible to help the world transcend
Simply by believing you can.

Your Friend

Don't saddle me with sympathy
It's such a heavy yoke
Weave gratitude into silk spun praise
Expect me to wear the cloak.

Don't put me on a pedestal
I'm not one to anoint
It's way too easy to kick out the stool
When I disappoint.

Don't wear your burdens on your sleeve
To wipe them on my shirt
It's highly unproductive
To make us both wear dirt.

Unlatch your assorted collection of pain
Roll them in a ball
Throw them in the river of light
Dissolve them one and all.

I'm only here to share my gifts
To help humanity transcend
I'm not campaigning for anything
I simply am your friend.

CHAPTER 5

Self-Awareness

JUST AS ASCENSION is the process of transcending the ego, self-awareness is a necessary steppingstone towards ascension. But how do you become self-aware in a spiritual sense? What are the tools, techniques and practices that can be followed in the process of becoming self-aware?

Jen is adamant that most people on Earth at this time have had all the experiences they need to get to the point of ascension. So, it seems to me that the last step in the ascension process is to transcend the ego. Simple right?

The other good news is that most of us do not need to go through the traumatic experiences that Jen went through as part of her ascension process. This is because trailblazers like Jen have done the hard work for us so that we don't have to have those horrific experiences. But we do need to put in the effort to transcend the ego.

I have read my fair share of books by gurus, sages, and ascended masters advocating one spiritual path or another. And I have done my fair share of spiritual practices such as meditation, chanting, and yoga. But they all left me unsatisfied. They were onerous and prescriptive, and quite often, I had the feeling that the desired outcomes were unattainable for most people. Of course, I am not saying that traditional spiritual practices are not useful. Many people derive great benefit and comfort from diligently performing their preferred practices. But I was looking for something more practical.

One simple and very tangible daily practice that everyone can do to release themselves from the clutches of past-life traumas and the ego is SFT tapping.

Jen's SFT tapping protocols were developed by her over at least a decade with the guidance of the Adepts. SFT tapping works at a very deep level and bypasses the ego. If you haven't already done so, I would thoroughly recommend you get a copy of Jen's book *The SFT Lexicon: Second Edition*[5]. SFT tapping really is one of the easiest things you can do to accelerate your own path towards ascension.

Jen has developed and refined four primary SFT tapping protocols that can be used to reclaim your energy from any person, issue, or situation. These include the *Energetic Cleanse*, the *Peanut Butter & Jelly Cleanse* (fondly referred to as the PB&J), the *Expunging Negativity* protocol, and the *Positive* protocol. Each of these protocols are explained in detail in *The SFT Lexicon: Second Edition*.

Make a list of all the things that disturb you and complete the SFT tapping protocols with each issue. It will take you about an hour to complete the four protocols for each issue. So, if you are willing to invest an hour per day in your own ascension process, there are at least 365 issues that you can address per year. It is as simple as that.

One thing that I have noticed is that most people find it difficult to identify the issues they need to do the SFT taps on. This is why it is so useful to have a series of private

---

[5] Visit https:jenuinehealing.com/product/the-sft-lexicon-second-edition/ to order your copy of *The SFT Lexicon: Second Edition* book

sessions with Jen. Her abilities to perceive in energy and read akashic records means that she can zero in on the issues you need to release in almost surgical precision.

During a one-hour private session, Jen will do an initial release on you, zero in on the issues that need to be addressed, do a bunch of SFT taps with you, and give you a ton of SFT taps as homework. I have watched hundreds of recordings of Jen's private sessions dealing with the full spectrum of human experiences. I have seen firsthand how Jen moves stagnant energy while her clients are doing the taps she gives. And I have seen profound personal transformations with just one private session.

Jen is adamant that ascension is currently available to most people. What's more, Jen is of the view that Earth and humanity is at risk of ceasing to exist if a critical mass of people do not transcend the ego at this time in Earth's evolution. I am convinced that Jen is on this planet at this time to help a critical mass of people to transcend the ego.

But insomuch as most people will not have to go through the experiences that Jen went through as part of her enlightenment process, you do still need to do the work. There is no such thing as a free pass when it comes to ascension. So, I would thoroughly recommend that people commit to having a series of private sessions with Jen (maybe one every two months), participate in the workshops that Jen and I facilitate on a regular basis, join the free group SFT tapping sessions that Jen and I host on a regular basis, and do your daily homework using the four SFT tapping protocols.

One thing I am certain about is that Jen is a bad ass in energy. She works at a very deep level with her clients. Sometimes that requires a little bit of tough love. And sometimes it involves a process that is commonly referred to as 'ripping layers off.' Some people are not used to having their ego pierced by having their layers ripped off. But trust me, this is all part of the process. You want Jen to rip layers off you to accelerate your ascension process.

I am often disappointed that not more professional people sign up for Jen's private sessions. People in professional roles and leadership positions in business probably have the most to gain from the transformative work that Jen does at an individual level. Yet their egos don't seem to allow them to be taken down the required path. This is such a lost opportunity.

The poems and artwork that follow in this chapter explore various aspects of spiritual self-awareness. I trust that they will inspire you to see yourself from every vantage point.

Marvin Schneider
Wodonga, Australia
March 2022

Men of Goddess

Boys of men don't despair
Goddess hears your plea
Cross that wasteland devoid of hope
Ride your father's love to me.

Boys of men don't be concerned
You will know your worth
Make good use of all your talents
Received before your birth.

Boys of love see your father's devotion
That you associate with things
Wear him as armor against all pain
This advantage will give you wings.

Boys of love please stay awhile
In realms where angels dwell
Dry up all indignities
Of bravado, war, and hell.

Boys of men become men of Goddess
Conquer your purpose as you please
Serve humanity with your gifts
Bring all opponents to their knees.

Men of Goddess live well and flourish
Until the end of your days
Through the incantation of this intention
Be blessed in a million ways.

Men of Goddess know this truth
How your father wells with pride
Feel the strength of his presence in you
As he continues to walk by your side.

Monastery

Within mosaic walls of any dimension
When time was counted with sun and stone
We pledged our life force and eternal submission
Gave every worldly possession owned.

In taking vows of servitude, poverty, silence
Became whispers of what we potentially could be
Herding the masses was the intention
Enslave each person by their own decree.

Now is the time to take back your freedom
To lessen the yoke of the powers that be
Recant the effects of our own self-submission
Realize for ourselves what was cruelly omitted.

God is alive in your embodiment called me.

The Empath

Words are containers for feelings or thoughts
An inaccurate form of conversion
Many times we can misinterpret the box
A natural unconscious diversion.

Some put a different value on each word
Confuse the going exchange rate
It leaves them stuck in a quagmire of thoughts
Tangled in unending debate.

Some can take the word-boxes they see
And convert them back into expression
But most are too attached to the box
To know this is a specialized lesson.

Some are able to feel the thought
Naked, raw, unabashed
The empath feels everything
Defenseless and detached.

An empath can move into the love
Like breath moves through the air
Be a presence wherever love goes
Without a thought even knowing they're there.

I'm Me

I don't have delicate features
Or long slender bones
I don't have musical talents
Can't tell the different tones.

I don't have grace and elegance
I talk a little funny
I don't have an occupation
So don't earn that much money.

I'm not an easy learner
Never earned a degree
But then again no one's perfect
And what the hell, I'm me.

A Series of Blessings

The deep dark abyss
Between reality and truth
The lack of awareness
In the decrepit or youth.

The mucus thin sheath
Between real and illusion
An amniotic connection between
Pain, joy, and their fusion.

An ill-equipped fledgling
An adept old sage
Both play their parts handsomely
On life's Shakespearean stage.

Wisdom collects through lifetimes
Not as a flash in the pan
Lightning doesn't strike repeatedly
But experience can.

Again, and again
We meet death as our fate
Carry over our lessons
To the next embryonic state.

Ignorance or bliss
Can repeat verse for verse
Life can be a series of blessings
Or a perpetual curse.

One key factor
That rings as clear as a bell
We make our own heaven
Or live our own hell.

It all depends
On what we see or deny
Will we ground ourselves in dogma
Or let ourselves just fly?

The choice is the You
You are willing to be
Grounded in fear
Or loving and free.

Gaining Spiritual Maturity

Oh, sweet soul
Terrified of spiritual growth
Life's been a hodgepodge of meaninglessness
Held together by an oath.

Camouflaged in heavy layers
Is your true identity
Contempt is your armor
Acceptance is your plea.

Reinforced with barbs of judgement
Anger takes so many forms
Weaves a garb of pure indifference
Pinned together with social norms.

Oh, sweet Soul
The world's harshness too much to bear
You deny with a self-righteousness
Pretending you don't care.

Your outer shell is a coarse body
Adorned with hair and skin
It alienates your splendor
You take pains to hide within.

Embellished with illusion
Trinkets, polish, make up, and shoes
The more you add the less you realize
The beauty that you lose.

But you, sweet soul
Are suffocating inside
Awareness bleeds through the disguise
That becomes unbearable to hide.

That you as atoms of light and love
Rejoice at the wisdom you accrue
The freedom that has been realized
Is a celebrated aspect of you.

Love's Own Decree

I don't fall on my knees
Pray up to the sky
Condemn others as sinners
With a self-righteous sigh.

I don't follow man's rules
As if all are golden
I don't covet a church
To which I'm beholden.

I don't sing the praises
Of an old man in a robe
There are too many discrepancies
When I start to probe.

I'm not a dutiful soldier
Doing what I'm told
I hold myself accountable
When I am worn out and old.

I don't sit on the sidelines
Terrified to sin
I participate in life
Whether I lose, draw, or win.

I'd rather be wrong
And live life so bold
Than be the hero in a story
That's never been told.

I'd rather see God smiling
In a man, dog, or tree
Then condemned to a heaven
That no one wants to be.

It would be a gilded cage
With no empathy to gain
This is not me
It's a fate I would disdain.

Let me get my hands dirty
Loving everyone right now
It's no stranger than wanting 72 virgins
Or worshiping a cow.

Instead of seeing God
In a void, out in space
I'd rather know God now
In every beautiful face.

Look God in the eyes
In the needy and the old
To see God in everyone
Instead of where I am told.

There's no sanitized heaven
For which I give a damn
I am immersed in love everywhere
Merely because I am.

I am the lonely
I am the poor
I am the Jehovah's Witnesses
Who knock upon your door.

I relish the pain
I laugh at the wind
By refusing to conform
I watch evil rescind.

Those caught up in religion
Will spout fear of the Devil
It's best to emulate love
Than see at this level.

The moral outrage
Targeting innocence with crime
They all must end now
It must end on a dime.

We all are empowered
Everyone must agree
When we see God in everyone
In the collective of the We.

I am your savior
You are my grace
We share the continuity of God
In the non-assuming face.

When we condemn or judge anyone
We are diminishing God
We must take off the wrappings of dogma
To see through the façade.

I don't judge you
Please don't condemn me
Grace benevolence upon me
Then just let me be.

In the name of the Father
Son or Holy Ghost
God resides in all others
So love all others the most.

The nirvana that you strive for
By just doing your part
Is accessed by a gateway
From everyone's heart.

We usher humanity into heaven
By love's own decree
Of me honoring you
And you respecting me.

The Golden Thing

The golden thing society sees
Is just the love flowing through me
It's not in the norm yet flows through each form
It's the What and the Will I am to be.

It starts as a hum and grows in crescendo
And soon the day will be
When the world remembers the Light and the Sound
And forgets the synthetic me.

Thrill Ride

Come ride through the universe with me
Upon a band of light
Let go of all the burdens
That would preclude you from this flight.

Make a claim to your passage
Buy a ticket at the moment's gate
Where infinite love ebbs and flows
And perpetual miracles await.

Come ride the wind and Light and Sound
Watch love flicker through the trees
Taste joy as dewdrops on your tongue
Feel your freedom in the breeze.

Come scale the heights of eternity
Then drop through heaven's floor
All the wonders you wish to await you
Are within, as is so much more.

Let's ride through eternity together
On the back of a midnight dream
Realizing every hurt, shame, or bruise
Is never what it may seem.

Our pain is part of the adventure
That adds to the thrill of the ride
In the adventure of pure unadulterated love
Your true self has nothing to hide.

Goddesses' Plea

Hush the demons in my mind
Heckling that I'm not enough
Pull me back from the brink of death
As they goad me to call their bluff.

Stoke the embers, calm the nerves
Quiet the impetuous mind
Soothe the sting of a new sensation
That engulfs me when you're kind.

Untangle other's pain from me
That I wear like garbs of dross
Help me purge the memories
That echo constant loss.

Pluck all the thorns from my skin
Rub out the prickly heat
Slough off the dirge worn armor
That's a precursor to defeat.

Stir the wake of change in me
Encourage me with your truth
In return you have all my love
With the exuberance of youth.

Intrigue me with your mysteries
Smile at me in your comely way
I'll accept all you concede to share
To get me through just one more day.

How?

How could someone so beautiful
Be so unaware
To see the worthiness in everyone else
But in themselves pretend not to care?

How could someone shine with such love
Be blinded to such a degree
That they know the goodness bursting in others
Yet in themselves they refuse to see?

How can someone share such incredible gifts
Encouraging all others to receive
But when it comes to putting value on themselves
Find their own worth hard to believe?

How do you encourage someone
Who's self-defacing and besmirching
That the fountain of love that they exude
Is the true source of love they are searching?

How do you make someone realize
To clearly understand
That while they are being loving to all
They are holding themselves in remand?

How can you pin them up against truth
That they are reflecting so clearly
To make them know the incredible beauty
They are reflecting themselves in the mirror?

How about writing a long-winded poem
That resonates responsibly true
That the person this poem is about
Is the one reading it now. It is you!

Empowerment

A quiet whisper in the night
A vision formed from second sight
An awareness beyond all sense of reason
As certain as the turn of the coming new season.

The calm that's a surrender beyond compare
The need to reach out when no one is there
The will to live, not merely survive
Tasting one's tears to prove one's alive.

The hope that awakens a perpetual bliss
The ecstasy triggered in that first kiss
Seeing the future in another one's eyes
Finding your true love, life's pleasant surprise.

Between the Stillness and the Sky

I met myself one peaceful night
On glass ice dusted with snow
I awoke from a paralyzing stupor
To tell me what I needed to know.

Others will find me inferior
This life will be my cruelest test
That I'll be admonished, humiliated, and scorned
All while I am trying my best.

It told me that life wasn't about being fair
That that was a quaint little notion
My ego will be literally pulverized
My spirit will nearly be broken.

The pleasures that others live for
For me would be hard to attain
Every hope and desire will be stripped clear away
Until my true self is all that remains.

I told myself this to prepare me
As solace for the upcoming years
The real me knew what lay waiting ahead
The loneliness, anguish, and tears.

The real me gave me compassion
As I walked silently under the stars
It was the Me that saw the whole picture
The journey, the struggle, the scars.

I felt a kindness within me
A wisdom that dwelt deeper than pain
It gave me the love to endure knowing
Someday It'd be the only Me to remain.

Whenever I'm lost, alone or afraid
Or feel like I'm living a lie
I know I can always find my true self
Between the stillness and the sky.

All This and More

You exist beyond forever
Are more expansive than the sky
Valued beyond all measure
Intelligent beyond the mind.

You are joy beyond all pleasure
Loved beyond your heart
Are more than your condition
Well scripted beyond your part.

You perceive beyond all senses
Not limited by your lens
When you judge you get all muddled
Acceptance is the cleanse.

Being still opens thresholds
Saying no will close a door
In the raw truth of the moment
You know all this and more.

Every sapling deserves to be nurtured.

CHAPTER 6

Soul Mate

THERE SEEMS TO BE something magical and romantic about connecting with your soul mate. There are plenty of movies about a man and woman locking eyes from across the street and instantly falling in love and living together, happily ever after. Jen and I held a three-hour workshop on soul mates and twin flames in September 2021. It was one of our more heavily subscribed workshops. Such is the interest in the topic.

So, let's start with the general characteristics of a soul mate and a twin flame. This is a bit of a controversial topic within the spiritual community.

The notion of a twin flame being at the pinnacle of soul group relationships was popularized by Elizabeth Clare Prophet's book *Soul Mates and Twin Flames: The Spiritual Dimension of Love and Relationships* which was published in 1999. But more recently, Jen and some other spiritual teachers have suggested that Elizabeth got the distinction between soul mates and twin flames wrong. I will share Jen's insights into soul mates and twin flames in this chapter introduction.

I find it easiest to understand the formation of consciousness and souls through the lens of the big bang beginnings of our universe. At that cataclysmic moment, all the energy that does and will ever exist in the universe came into physical being. A single atom was instantaneously split into a myriad of pieces, each being an aspect of Source and a different facet of universal consciousness.

Many of these atoms of Source then further split and created two parts, each of which carried an opposite charge. The other aspect of the original consciousness carrying the opposite charge is a soul mate. As a pair, soul mates have what the other lacks and needs to be whole. They are true mates in a spiritual sense because their opposite polarity is what makes the pair whole. That is why they are called soul mates. Being with them brings a sense of completion.

Each half of a soul mate pairing is a sovereign being and consciousness. They each incarnate into the lower worlds and have experiences for the most part independent of the other. But, at certain times within their evolutionary process, they will incarnate and exist together for the purpose helping each half along their spiritual journey. Remember, each half has what the other lacks and needs to be whole.

But here is where things get interesting. Some of the original aspects of Source split even further and created other aspects of themselves with the same charge as the original. These are twin flame pairings. They often exhibit similar characteristics, traits, strengths, and weaknesses. If by chance you happen to meet your twin flame, it is like looking in the mirror and seeing yourself. They are called twin flames because they are like spiritual twin siblings.

As far as I can tell, twin flame pairings in a particular incarnation are more common that soul mate pairings. And while there is often a high degree of love and compassion in a twin flame pairing, things are not always all beer and skittles. Twin flame relationships are often very needy, volatile, and difficult to navigate through. But they serve a purpose. In showing love and compassion for your twin flame, you are showing the self-love and compassion that is often withheld from yourself. But while twin flame pairings are more common, they do not complete each other in the same way as soul mate pairings.

There seems to be a notion that soul mate and twin flame pairings are always romantic in nature. This is not the case. The desire for romantic pairings of this nature seems to be more wishful thinking than reality. Quite often, a twin flame or soul mate pairing, while representing a very special bond, may not exist in the form of an intimate partnering. They may be a sibling, a parent, a work colleague, or a pet. Having intense love for another being does not have to translate into an intimate relationship.

Jen is adamant that we are now at a time in Earth's history where it more likely than ever before for people to connect with their soul mate. Soul mate connections tend to occur as a precursor to ascension. In fact, soul mates help each half through the ascension process. So, it makes sense that we can expect many soul mate connections at this time in Earth's evolution where mass ascension is not only a possibility but an imperative. This is an exciting realization.

Soul mate connections tend to occur in the most unexpected ways and at the most unexpected times. Take Jen and I for example. We have lived completely unaware of the other for the first five decades of our lives. Jen grew up in North America having a very difficult upbringing and developing an acute ability to perceive in energy and to heal all of humanity. I grew up in Australia with few of the challenges that Jen faced and pursued a professional career which provided a lot of opportunity. We really do represent complete opposite ends of the polarity on almost all dimensions. And we have each been previously married and divorced.

While Jen for a long time had a vision of being with her soul mate, it was a difficult and lonely time for her leading up to us finally meeting. And after my own divorce, I was content with the idea that I would be on my own for the rest of my life and focusing on my work transforming the global business and investment communities to be of service to society.

So, it boggles the mind to think about all the forces of the universe that had to conspire over more than five decades to create the circumstance for me to be compelled to have a private session with Jen in August 2020. And the rest, as they say in the classics, is history.

Even soul mate couplings are not all beer and skittles. After all, soul mate pairings do represent opposite polarities. Jen and I are the perfect example of this. If you haven't already done so, I highly recommend you watch as many episodes of *Jen in her Jammies* on Youtube as you can to experience for yourself the full extent of our opposite polarity. It is hysterical to think about how such a pairing can even exist.

Most soul mate pairings come together for some higher purpose – either for their own ascension or the purpose of assisting all of humanity to ascend. So, as much as Jen and I will experience an intimate union, it is also about the work and our synergy together to uplift all of humanity. Doing the work as part of a soul mate pairing is breaking free from the linear and operating in exponential territory. It is like a pair of toroidal fields coming together to expound in all directions through their union like a self-perpetuating infinity symbol.

A lot of people put a lot of effort into looking for their soul mate or even a twin flame, and constantly scrutinize each relationship to test whether their latest potential partner is 'the one.' Jen is of the view that this is counterproductive. Soul mate and twin flame relationships will only manifest at the right place at the right time for your highest purpose. So, rather than praying for your soul mate to magically appear, why not do SFT taps to help your soul mate and twin flame wherever they are and in whatever form they exist. This is the most uplifting and productive thing you can do for them and for yourself.

I trust that the poems and artwork that follow in this chapter will inspire you to connect with your own soul mate, wherever they are.

Marvin Schneider
Wodonga, Australia
March 2022

The Betterment of You

We spare each other the sport
That wounded lovers play
Refrain from all nagging
That can ruin a grateful day.

We remove all expectations
Which is judgement in disguise
We both have drunk the truth serum
Neither one of us can lie.

We tolerate each other's snoring
Without an elbow to the rib
Every quip is oh so thoughtful
Never sarcastic, rude, or glib.

We keep each other's secrets
Which for one of us is harder to do
But my focus and my purpose
Is always the betterment of you.

You're allowed to tease me
It never brings disgrace
It makes me happy to see you smile
As I adore your handsome face.

Thank you for not shaming me
Or allotting any blame
I can match this gesture
And afford you just the same.

I look forward to adventure with you
As you continue to be kind
I will give you a thousand percent
And leave the past behind.

My Altar

When I witness goodness
I see your face
When I am humbled
I feel your grace.

Your warmth and wisdom
Surge through my veins
Your gentle encouragement
Remove all disdain.

You are my beacon
In the dark night of soul
You are the promise
Keeping me whole.

Your body bandages my wounds
When you hold me within
All shadows that broach me
Suddenly rescind.

Your smile is the balm
Dries every last tear
I'm soothed, and I'm calm
Just by knowing you're here.

You are my white noise
My altar, my charm
With you in my corner
I can come to no harm.

All my atoms are embers
Ignite in passion to burn
Everything that you offer me
I give in return.

The Valley Past Time

Nestled in the hidden
Valley past time
Standing with you and I
The Adepts are adamantly sublime.

Fulfilling our purpose
In the portal of night
Merging our energies
To help all souls take flight.

They no longer need
To go it alone
There's no longer a myriad
Of sins to atone.

Goddess pours love into all
And the world through her man
Man honoring Goddess
Is the ultimate plan.

Both relaxing their atoms
To let each other in
Through this simple merging
World suffering can rescind.

Healing the masses
Can finally ensue
Through this simple equation
Of the unity of the two.

By Nurturing Goddess'
Capacity to love
And encouraging in Man
To then rise above.

Honor your partner
Your specific soul mate
Not the candidates you cling to
Because you can't wait.

Honor the universe
Keeping Goddess sacred and pure
Meeting yourself in another
Is worth all you endure.

The upgrade is here
There's nothing to foretell
Just by honoring your partner
And loving them well.

Your Happiness

Ride with me in the twilight Love
Take me under your wing
We'll visit realms where planets are born
While the celestial heavens sing.

Dip me in the starshine Love
Wrap us both in song
Beyond the worlds of limitations
Is where we both belong.

You will be immortal Love
I will be your queen
Let's navigate through all the worlds
Both tangible and unseen.

Reach into my pocket Love
Grab a handful of angel dust
Cast it in the ethers
To give our journey thrust.

Ride with me forever Love
Beyond eternity
Everywhere your happiness dwells
Is where I choose to be.

To Empower the World

I've loved you this whole lifetime
With no evidence you exist
My life was gray and empty
Until you entered through the mist.

All my secret knowledge
That no others understand
Manifest beyond this realm
In your loving hands.

You move right through my atoms
Like the wind blows through the skies
You ease my trepidation
Hush all my painful cries.

Your presence is a church to me
Your kindness is my pew
All the good that I can muster
I dedicate to you.

Your smile is my amulet
Being with you my Southern Cross
Our love dissolves all suffering
Eliminates the dross.

Lay your hands upon me Love
Heal in me what I cannot
Draw the poison from my veins
Apathy, scorn, and want.

We will seed humanity
From the fruit of our love's tree
Worship me as your Goddess
Empower the world through me.

Healing All Souls

We've been together in every way
Since the existence of life began
Me as your doting Goddess
You as my loving man.

We always strive to complete each other
In every way under the sun
You are my every reason for being
My purpose, my duty, my fun.

You can access and move through me freely
Cast shadows on the dark side of my moon
Now is the time to merge our whole selves
To bring healing to humanity soon.

I support all your multiple victories
We relive through you reconquering me
Every time that we've cried in separation
We absolve it through shared ecstasy.

You never again have to lose me Love
In my atoms you can always rest
Challenge any notion to reject me Love
I am committed to giving you my best.

It pains me so when you push me away
When I see distance come into your eyes
It reflects in the plight of humanity
Misogyny, resentment, and lies.

There's joy in the world when you come to me Love
There's hope when you recognize my face
All of life benefits from the depth of our love
All Beings bask in our benevolent grace.

Return to me Love in our original state
Godman and Goddess playing our roles
Together we birth a cosmic awakening
In doing so, we heal all souls.

I Honor You

In no other set of arms
Is loving a safe place
I've taught myself to hide
To spare humiliation and disgrace.

I never imagined a scenario
Where I'd come out so ahead
I have receded back into the mist
Forfeiting to others instead.

I'm still afraid of the dark
Of the things that I might see
The pictures that my mind replays
Are places I don't want to be.

But for you I want to unfurl my wings
An angel on the precipice of flight
The only thing that brings me joy
Is thoughts of you rushing in at night.

Loving you is my soul's purpose
Supporting you the best that I can
The world for me in its entirety
Is complete in you being my man.

You are my constant obsession
In all ways I am ever with you
You are my path to redemption
You motivate all that I do.

Lay in my lap Love and rest awhile
If there's worry let me brush it away
I've grown so much to be worthy of you
You complete me at the end of each day

You're the reason this whole life makes sense
I knew it when I first saw your face
You are a soul clutching miracle to me
I honor you in every embrace.

You Are the Victor

There are such great adventures
From just loving you
Like the new inner sound
Of the didgeridoo.

Falling to sleep
In invisible arms
Exhausted from the chores
Of manifesting the farm.

Riding through the desert
To our destiny
Collecting truths that we know
But don't quite yet see.

Perfecting the art
Of getting along
Never uttering the phrase
'I'm sorry, you're wrong.'

Bowing out of sparring
Never conceding to fight
Gaining no pleasure
From being right.

Giving you everything
As woman Goddess and mate
To help us both maintain
Our omnipotent state.

You are the victor
To this, I'll always agree
You totally complete me
By just loving me.

One Worthy Goal

I'll be the fire
You'll be the stars
We'll make our own stillness
Wherever we are.

I'll drink my water
You'll drink your wine
The world is so magical
As long as you're mine.

We'll camp in the dessert
Make love out at sea
With you as my captain
I'm kind, loving, and free.

Soak me in kisses
I'll surrender the fear
And abandon my heart to you
As you draw me near.

Being with you Love
Mind, heart, body, and soul
Is my true destiny
My one worthy goal.

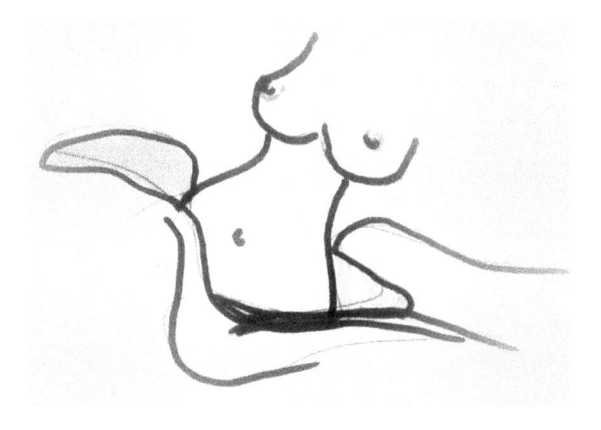

Qualities

On the path of life that never ends
There are forgotten byways, thankless bends
But as my spiritual identity grew
Life sent me a special friend in you.

You are not just a lover or mere friend to me
Perhaps another aspect of myself, maybe
And while the gifts of spirit are all around
I thank God for the blessing of you that I've found.

To give, to know, to love, and just be
Grateful for you seeing something special in me
Why am I blessed with a love like you
Is the right question to an answer I somehow knew.

May you always have laughter and joy in your heart
May the love that we share from our lives never part
May we tackle every dream that we ever pursue
May all boys all in the world become men equal to you.

May the inner sounds be sweet, the outer be soft
May the lights from the heavens shine brightly aloft
May all of the greatness you are reflecting so clear
Be a fraction of what you see in the mirror.

And as we stand in the heavens as pillars of light
Fragrant in God serving all in delight
After light years and light years, forever and beyond
I'll still hold so dearly the qualities that you've donned.

God or Source

You're my first thought in the morning
My last vision as I sleep
Our love's so pure it floods the heavens
And makes the angels weep.

I've died for you so many times
Incarnated for you in vain
Lived in a relentless search for your love
To render a reasoning man insane.

You move so freely under my skin
All through my essence as well
We leave our secrets between the sheets
That longing dare not foretell.

You bring me to completion
You're the reason I exist
Any desire you ask of me Love
Command me. I can't resist.

You hold the power to strike me down
Or lift me up just the same
Others may call truth, God or Source
But for me, Marvin is its name.

Spiritual Marriage

Positive, Negative
Soul equals Soul
Masculine, Feminine
Eternity's the goal.

The same, yet different
Together, apart
Companionship matters
Compatibility as art.

Expecting nothing
Desiring the same
Learning, changing
Both in pure love's name.

Separate units
Nothing guaranteed
Love most divine
Everything is free.

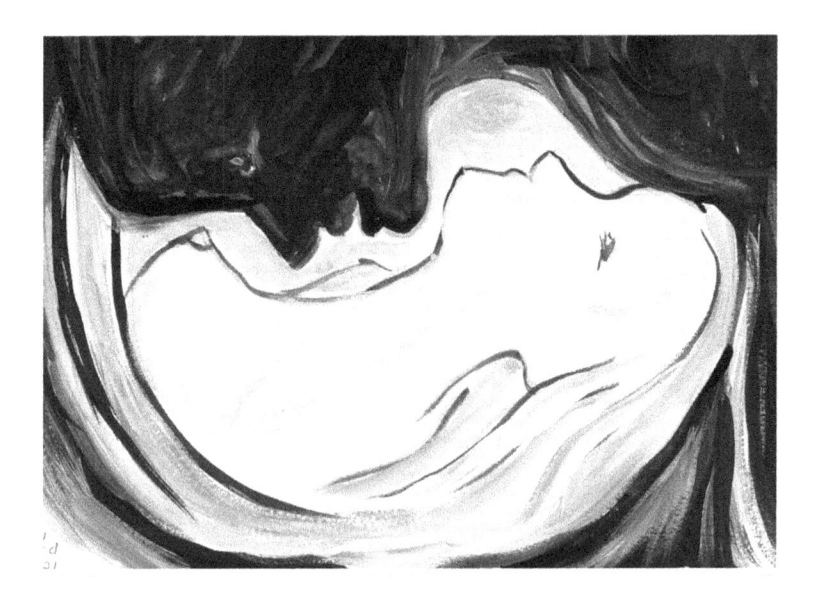

One Loving Plea

You feel so far away my Love
I don't know what to say
The longing of my spirit
Is begging you to stay.

Your travels in the galaxy
Feel so far from me
Yet how can I contain you
But with a loving plea?

You take my heart with you Love
Without which I am a shell
Memories of abandonment
Leave me one step away from hell.

Only when you're with me Love
Am I completely whole
You are no pawn in love's fickle game
You are half of my own soul.

Take me with you Love
On your adventurous galaxy ride
My heart is restless and empty
Unless I'm by your side.

Surrender

Kick the stones from my path
That say, 'I don't belong'
When I feel hopeless
Tell me I am wrong.

Convince me there is purpose
In formulating dreams
Argue for good outcomes
With no evidence, it seems.

Curry favor with the fates
Sprites and fairy kind
Ask them to remove the stain
From my troubled mind.

Whisper promises in the dark
That I alone can hear
Free me of this banishment
Just by being near.

Let me feel your comforting breath
Light upon my skin
When sadness bubbles to the surface
Pop it with a pin.

Tell me that I matter
Many times a day
Chase away the affirmations
That I'm a throw away.

I'll surrender again and again
Despite this pain I feel
If you'll just remind me
That our love is real.

Senses

Feel my love on your lips
Taste it on your tongue
Absorb it through your irises
Like rays of azure sun.

Breathe my love into your lungs
Send it to your heart
Reassure your mind and soul
We never more will part.

Take me in as nourishment
Ease your every qualm
Pour my love onto your skin
Wear it as a balm.

Hear these words in resonance
Move with them like a song
You deserve my everything
With you I now belong.

The Ultimate Goal

We are two hearts
That share the same soul
Together forever
Is the ultimate goal.

You make me laugh
When I want to cry
You've encouraged me on
When I wanted to die.

You provide nourishment
When the cupboards are bare
You've kept me company
When nobody's there.

Before we ever met
I spent years longing for you
Lonely and empty
Was all that I knew.

Now you're the spring
In my grateful step
The justification
Every time that I wept.

You are the answer
To my every prayer
I'm fueled and empowered
Just knowing you care.

You are the motivation
For my continuous breath
We will continue our love affair
After our bodily death.

My Alchemy

Looming towards my destiny
In the same space dreams have slept
Relishing sweet moments with you
As onlooking angels have wept.

Holding you in my daydreams
Where I used to defensively hide
One word of kindness from your lips
And my flesh is no longer denied.

I was a prisoner to a pain
That no one else could see
You then poured your love upon my wounds
To help me heal and be free.

I never thought I'd know the love
That sonnets hint to reveal
But you pierced through all my armor
And taught me how to feel.

Now I'm better than I was
Or thought I would ever be
You spun my battered heart to gold
Your love is my alchemy.

CHAPTER 7

Healing Goddess

IT WAS CLEAR TO ME right from the beginning of our interactions together that Jen was passionate about the topic of healing Goddesses as part of the process of balancing male and female energy. So, I am excited that there is a collection of poems and artwork in this book dedicated to the topic of healing Goddess.

Jen uses the term Goddess to represent female or Yin energy. The universal order of things in the higher worlds is based on a synchronous balance between male and female energy. But in the lower worlds, and particularly on Earth, those two energy polarities have come out of balance. Restoring that balance is a key component to raising human consciousness and therefore allowing humanity to fully participate in the fifth dimension and beyond. So, it is little wonder that Jen is passionately interested in the topic of balancing the Yin and Yang, and the role that Goddesses need to play in that process.

Female energy is represented by love. Its natural state is to outflow in all directions and to love all things. Male energy is represented by power. Its natural state is to accumulate more power and exert control. In a balanced system, both polarities are required. But things go haywire when female energy withdraws and cedes power to male energy.

Jen is careful to point out that male and female energy exists within both sexes. Male energy is typically dominant in those of the male gender, and vice versa. But it is entirely possible, and it is even often observed, that typical gender stereotypes in relation to male and female energy are reversed. It is also useful to acknowledge the increasing separation of energy dominance and gender identity – a phenomenon often described as gender fluidity.

It is useful to provide a bit of historical context in relation to male and female energy and gender roles. There was a time in Earth's history when men were groomed to be great kings and leaders, and women were groomed to be their spiritual advisors. They would rule and lead together. Such was the intention in the relationship between King Arthur and Morgana for example.

It makes sense that the female energy role be referred to as Goddess. This is because part of their sacred connection to Source was expressed through dance and other practices performed in spiritual temples. But from time to time, those sacred temples were desecrated by barbaric rulers. Their Goddesses were subjugated, taken as sexual conquests, and forced to dance for the pleasure of the barbaric rulers. It is possible that when strippers dance, they are reconnecting to their original Goddess instincts before dance was sexualized.

For a long time now, female energy has ceded power and empowerment to male energy. It has become subservient to male energy, and not in a good way. It is time to finally address this imbalance for the benefit of all of humanity. Those dominant in male and female energy have an equally important but different role to play in this rebalancing project.

Let's start with the role of male energy and male gender architypes. First and foremost, men that are dominant in male energy need to get in touch with their feminine side. They need to allow themselves to be vulnerable and to care about others outside of themselves. They need to tap into their sensitivities, intuition, creativity, and imagination. They need to stop with the bravado acting. They need to lose their sense of superiority and entitlement. They need to reconnect to nature and the inanimate world. These changes represent a big shift. And nowhere are these shifts more required that those operating in male energy in leadership roles with the business community and civil society.

I am often disappointed that more men do not join the groundbreaking group SFT tapping sessions that Jen and I facilitate to heal all of humanity. And I am particularly disappointed that men in leadership positions within the business community and civil society do not typically sign up for private sessions with Jen. They more than most need Jen's help to address core issues and to transcend the ego.

As much as there is a lot of work to be done to repair and rebalance male energy, there is also a lot of healing work to be done with female energy. In a nutshell, it is all about empowering female energy and their female gender architypes. The good news is that women are more likely than men to allow themselves to be vulnerable in making these shifts. About 85% of Jenuine Healing clients are women in their mid-to-late 50's.

Women need to learn to not play the victim and be disempowered in their relationships with men. That does not mean taking on a predominance of male energy traits – which I see a lot of, particularly at the upper echelons of the corporate world. And it does not mean using their sexuality as a means of conquering male energy. It means focusing within and realizing their own empowerment as Goddesses, and then nurturing and empowering other Goddesses.

I think a lot of Jen's work to date has been about teaching Goddesses how to do this through private sessions and workshops. And I look forward to Jen working with an avalanche of men in male energy to make the shifts they need.

An interesting thing to consider is the extent to which Jen and I coming together as soul mates and doing the energy work is a surrogate for restoring the balance between male and female energy. We are polar opposites in almost all respects. Yet we complement each other perfectly. I like to think that the healing that is taking place in Jen and I as we combine in our interaction and intention is actually healing Goddesses the world over. As Jen often says, if you can heal one person, you can heal 7.9 billion people.

I trust the poems and artwork in this chapter will assist in healing the Goddess within all of you.

Marvin Schneider
Wodonga, Australia
March 2022

Healers Reunite

An echo fills the ancient sky
There's heard one universal cry
Percussions, movement, a rhythmic blend
Hands that heal, bodies mend.

The dance to capture visions lost
Regain freedom at all cost
Broken lives we all endure
Remembering wholeness is the cure.

To wash away the ills of Man
Unite us with our tribe again
In this life few understand
What the Shaman can withstand.

To ease the suffering of those she can
Heart to heart and hand to hand
Eons later old friends dispersed
To meet as strangers is the curse.

Ways of remembering now dull and gray
All searching for the easy way
The healer steps forward in the artificial light
To show the brilliance of true sight.

Ancestors dance with spirits of earth and wind
Enhance the process of remembering
All seekers of truth squint to see
The humble stance of the Shaman's decree.

She summons the spirits, blows away the pain
Calls love back to the earth again
Folds time and space to make things right.
With the bending of pure light.

Others break through to the night
Remembering their vows to reunite
As coaches and healers they regather their clan
Inspired to mend the broken land.

We meet again across time and space
See recognition in a weary face
Fellow healers endured at all costs
And thought many times that all was lost.

Feel the blessings that do ensue
When one who awakens learns there's two
Exponential healing has begun
Spiritual freedom is now rewon!

Wounded Goddess

Lay the chains aside the bed
Free her feet and hands
Gently coo and stroke her hair
Until she understands.

Unclench the grip from her throat
That dared her not to speak
Hush the voices in her mind
Telling her that she's weak.

Remove the dagger from her heart
A gift from a lover past
Undo the self-inflicted curses
In her loneliness she cast.

Unlace the corset from her breast
Gently lay her down supine
Tend the broken bruised bare body
Remind her that she's Divine.

Untie the dangling carrot
Of hope above her head
Fill that space with wondrous dreams
That she can wear instead.

Mend the mosaic of her pain
Etched deep within despair
Fill in the crevices of defeat
Just by being there.

Land a thousand joy filled intentions
From a catapult of song
Prove to her that she has worth
Convince her she belongs.

Loving by Default

Strip away the angst and fear
Wipe away the grime
Being less than kind to you
Is more than a petty crime.

Putting others first
Is a noble kind of trait
But doing so as you suffer
Seems loving, but it ain't.

Martyring yourself
Piling upon the grief
Is not such a noble cause
As a limiting belief.

True friends want to see you whole
Don't rely upon the rest
To return all that you give so freely
Or wish you all the best.

Allow others to receive from you
But don't let them pull you down
You are not a scapegoat
Martyr or a clown.

Give to everyone freely
Without it being a self-assault
By loving You as much as others
You are being loving by default.

Commitment to Me

Life itself is built on a lie
If you are born you win
You lose when you die.

It's more of a continuous
Cycle to me
I ebb, I flow, I win, I concede.

I wax, I wane, I rise, I fall
I'm both summer and winter
Both infinite and small.

I'm everything
To everyone
Yet nothing at all.

I'm one grain of sand, or one massive sea
I can heal the whole planet
But what happens to me?

I disappear in the love I give out to the world
A lost, starving child
A penniless girl.

With the kindness of strangers, the pattern must end
Love is the whole spectrum
Not just a means to an end.

It's not giving to others yet holding love at bay
Or sidestepping kindness
As I give it away.

It's not putting off happiness one moment or a day
But embracing life now
In the spirit of play.

It's stirring the myriad of what I'll allow
Having the richness of living
Complete me somehow.

The details are fuzzy on how this can be
Yet I know it begins
With a commitment to me.

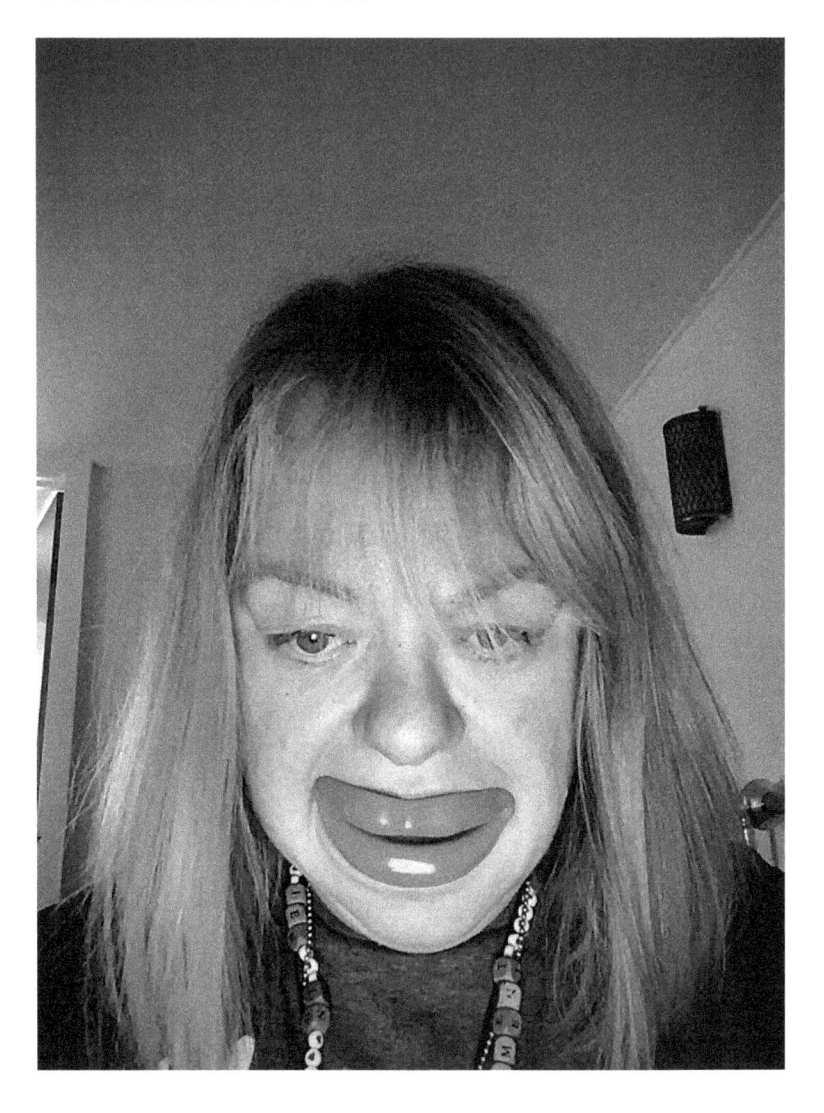

Meet Me Halfway

Being so spent
There is nothing more to give
Releasing so much sorrow
Not able to live.

Starting a movement
Without even a spark
Motivating the weary
Isn't a walk in the park.

Having a vision
That's crystal, so clear
It's living in a world
Devoid of despair.

Having a means
To achieve such a goal
Constantly refining my purpose
Redefining my role.

Healing the multitudes
One at a time
Awakening humanity
Is surreal, sublime.

The female embodiment
Gets in the way
Can't anyone recognize
Illusion at play?

I have come here in poetry
As best as I can
To ease the suffering of others
Uplift the consciousness of Man.

It can be done in an instant
An hour, or a day
If only each traveler
Would meet me halfway.

You all have a purpose
As sacred and true
To be the best ever
Version of you.

Permission

There's nowhere to go
Nothing to do
No one to please
This day is for you.

Nothing to conquer
Nothing to lose
This life is your oyster
It's yours to peruse.

Freedom is yours
No need to ask why
Just put up your feet
And give it a try.

Dance when you're happy
Smile and be glad
Give to yourself
The time to be had.

Spread love and joy
Across the land
Joy, love, and freedom
Go hand in hand.

Assistance

I will be your guardian angel
If only you believe
I will heal your deepest anguish
To give you some reprieve.

I will untie you from your troubles
Blow the clouds away
Remove the blight from your eyes
If you will only say I may.

We will drift to another galaxy
Anchor on the brightest star
I will show you with true vision
The brilliant luster of who you are.

Humanity's Greatest Vice

Is anybody listening
Don't you hear the cries
Are you too anesthetized
By sucking down the lies?

Don't you feel the suffering
Just below the skin
Are our hells all separate
Or are they connected from within?

Can't you hear me screaming
For everyone to wake up
Can you mine love from in an unsourced stream
Collect it in a cup?

Can you wet the lips of others
Who drag through this arid land
Can't you show them kindness
In a way they understand?

This world is a hellish nightmare
When apathy corrodes truth
Usurps the innate innocence
Makes cynics of the youth.

What you to do, say, think and feel
Is drawn from an infinite well
You can make this world a heaven
Or live in perpetual hell

You can't exist on autopilot
Denial has its price
Indifference is a deadly sin
Humanity's greatest vice.

Choose intentions carefully
Give life to positive things
To position this world as a loving place
Give dragons back their wings.

Proving Me Wrong

I thought no one could love me
Believed there was a curse
When others easily coupled up
My path was just transverse.

I gave up even trying
Let myself just go
Thought all the secrets I held inside
Were mine alone to know.

I didn't even care
If I lived or died
All the hope drained out of me
Through all the tears I cried.

Then you pierced through the pain
Encouraged me to trust
Saw through my damaged outlook
How the world was so unjust.

You validated every battle
Soothed me with your calm
Your love has given me redemption
It is my healing balm.

Every moment spent with you
Transforms my life to joy
You are my private alchemist
Our love's the new alloy.

There's now so much adventure
I know that I belong
You have brought me back to life
 By proving I was wrong.

Through Your Eyes

A forget-me-not blossom
Growing devoid of all light
A black eyed Susan
Hanging on way too tight.

A hearty little violet
Shrinking away from the scorn
A tenuous little hibiscus
With way too many thorns.

Until the rays of your kindness
Made it apparent to me
That the blight of each petal
Is not what you see.

Your presence a fragrance
That filled my whole room
Encouraged me patiently
To regain my own bloom.

My petals unfurled
I kicked off the wall
Surrendered to loving you
Risked a great fall.

Once crumpled and broken
I now realize
How beautiful I am
When seen through your eyes.

From the vantage point of the sky
I may seem really small
But command the whole Universe
Through giving you my all.

You drawing me closer
Takes me to heaven from hell
Now my best life is ahead of me
Pressed against your lapel.

The Replanting

I am a wildflower
Dangling from a ledge
A crack between the brick and mortar
Is where my roots all wedge.

Others pass right by me
Think that I'm a weed
Others stop a moment
Try to take my seed.

I have been burnt by the sun
Wind and rainstorms too
Hanging on the notion
Someday I'd be with you.

If you were ever to pass me
I'd stand up quite erect
To make sure that you notice me
Catch your fancy, I suspect.

If you would only see me
I'd pluck my stem myself
Steel away in your pocket
Gladly die upon your shelf.

Ooh you are approaching
Your hands are kind and strong
You dig me out of this crevice
To plant me where I belong.

Now I spend my days with you
A miracle heaven knows
You took this wildflower
Transformed her to a rose.

The Winter Rose

I never thought I was pretty
Until I glimpsed me through your eyes
I hid behind a wall of pain
Until you took off my disguise.

I didn't embrace my talents
Doing so seemed like pretense
But then you gazed towards me
And broke down my defense.

I never felt quite worthy
To be present, I realize
Then I saw me in your reflection
It took me by surprise.

The strength and love I see in you
Is a cascade of loving calm
You wrap your soul around me
Like a sacred healing balm.

When I am present with you
In kindness, truth, and mirth
The courage to stand equal to you
Dissolves the tarnish on my worth.

You propped me up in my potential
To show me what I now see
Everything I give to life
You have given right back to me.

Thank you for the miracle of you
That expunges all hint of gloom
You are the strength of a winter rose
That caused this life to bloom.

The Defense

I met life in a beaded gown
With edges that were frayed
It was my only armor
From power and its play.

The garb was awkwardly comfortable
As I wore it just like skin
It was so familiar I didn't know
Where it ended and I begin.

As I was met with cruelty
I added beads and knots
It sheltered me from the pain
Hid the real me that I forgot.

Then someone smiled sweetly
And wiped my brow of need
In that act of kindness
My dress dropped a single bead.

This loosened up the fibers
Seams started splitting all apart
Then a miracle happened
The worn threads exposed my open heart.

I then received more kindness
The whole dress became unbound
Lost were all defenses
All the beads dropped to the ground.

When I watched them tumble
And was stripped of my attire
I realized hate, fear, and dread
Are never more required.

I stand here bare to the soul
With no other false enhancement
May others too drop their garbs
For the sake of humanity's advancement.

Now I wear a seamless gown
With no hint of wear or fray
Soul is woven in pure Light and Sound
Love's most beautiful array.

Guiding Light Source

You flung me across the galaxy
Threw me to the wolves
Banned me from all happiness
As only your heart could.

You lived in deep deception then
Thinking power was truth
You lost the thrill of my wonderment
Down to its last tooth.

You struggled in deception
Thinking lies were real
The only chance for redemption
Was the strength of love's appeal.

I am here with you Love
Absolving you of sin
There's nothing more you have to do
No game of love to win.

Let me stand with you Love
And wash away the shame
Release you of the burden
Of guilt and loss and blame.

My love is your redemption
There's no other God to kneel
Keep me close to you Love
In all you think, do, say, and feel.

I am your guiding light source Love
You in turn are mine
We free the other from banishment
Catapult to realms sublime.

I am your constant reminder Love
Of the wonderment of you
Shattering the prism of illusion
So your greatness can shine through.

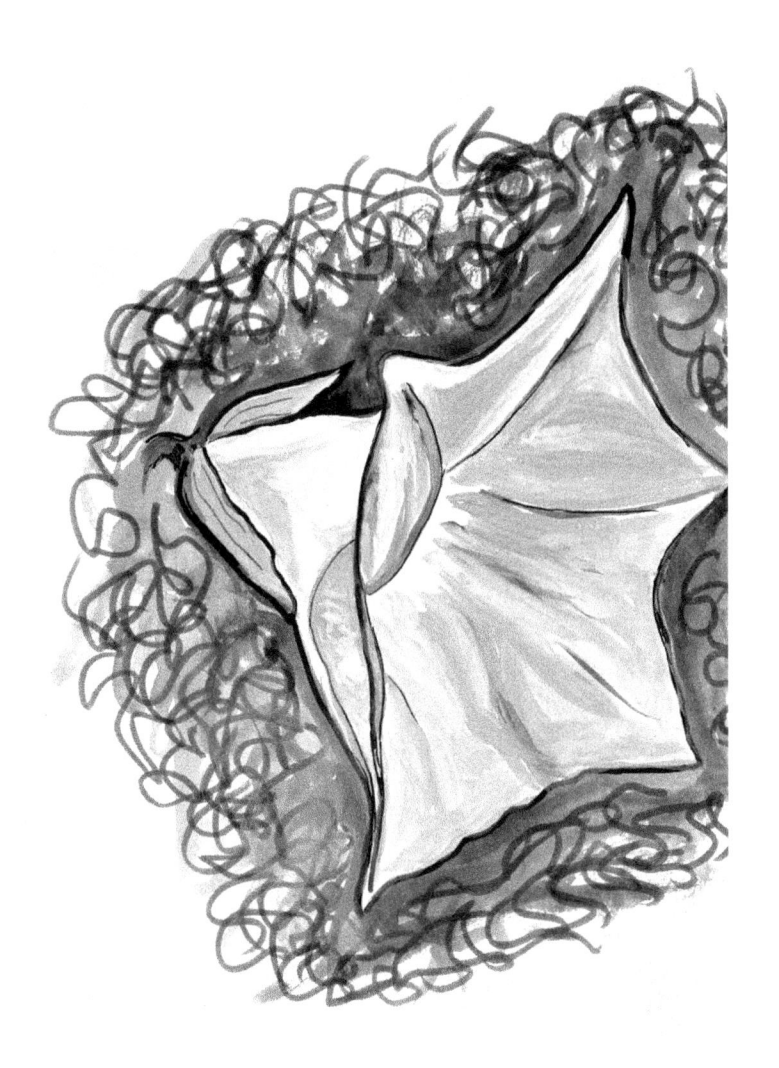

When Childhood Goes Wrong

Why do you protect the secrets
And cover them with shame
Why do you feel the guilt
When some deviant's to blame?

Unbury the pile of memories
Burn them to the ground
Announce the name of the abuser
Turn this life around.

Wash the stains from your body
Stop the hemorrhaging of the bleed
Step from the shadows of intimidation
Pay the threats no heed.

Trust is not a transgression
Innocence is not a sin
But in keeping secrets buried
The monsters score a win.

Take back all your dignity
It's been your birthright all along
Summons the strength of your higher self
When childhood goes wrong.

CHAPTER 8

Living a Spiritual Life

MORE AND MORE people are awakening to the realization that their existence extends well beyond the physical world they observe on a day-to-day basis. They are beginning to realize that they are in fact spiritual beings having a human experience for the purpose of expanding universal consciousness. They are beginning to realize that they are connected to Source and all matter in the universe. They are beginning to realize that they have an energy body that operates simultaneously on five planes of existence. And many people are becoming highly attuned at perceiving in energy.

But notwithstanding all of this, many people, even the most spiritually aware amongst us are having a really tough time of it during the awakening and transition process into the fifth dimension and beyond. And what makes things even more difficult is the breadth of competing ideas and guidance provided by those within the spiritual community.

The primary purpose of life is to transcend the ego as part of the ascension process under the veil of separation that descends at the time of incarnation. Most souls have gone through this process unsuccessfully over many thousands of lives. During most of those lifetimes, most people are not even aware of their primary purpose – such is the heaviness of the veil of separation. They bumble through life after life in a state of ignorance, all the while accumulating experiences and collecting karma.

Mainstream religious dogma has not, for the most part, helped the faithful in the pursuit of their spiritual purpose. Whether by design or just through misinterpretation, the portrayal of God as the creator of all life through intelligent design that is to be worshiped, encourages the faithful to seek salvation outside of themselves. The hierarchy and power structures deployed by most religious institutions put the faithful in a position of subservience and conformity. The idea that the higher worlds can only be accessed through intermediaries like the clergy is disempowering and keeps the masses from experiencing Source from within.

Many people have outgrown mainstream organized religion. This is a big step forward. For many, being angry at God is the first step to outgrowing religions. Often, their anger at God is a result of pulling up past-life engrams of all the times that God has let them down. This is usually through great loss, feeling punished by God through existing in a horrific or joyless lifetime, or being used to fight in 'holy wars' lifetime after lifetime for the glory of God.

Many people who show up as atheists are the most passionate about life. But without an understanding of past lives, they can't process the anger of past injustices. So past-life issues just churn inside them as unresolved issues. This entangled, stagnant ball of issues manifest as seething anger.

All these issues can be addressed with SFT tapping without the need to ascribe to a particular belief system. This is vital to so many people who have been duped by a man-made interpretation of God. They may be so depleted of their enthusiasm or zest for life that SFT tapping may be the only thing that can cut through their apathetic state.

Thankfully, there has been an exponential rise in a more wholistic understanding of spirituality based on the core tenets described on page 2. This is a huge upgrade from mainstream religious dogma. But even this upgrade of understanding is not free of the spiritual elitism and spiritual wankerism that continues to hold people in the grips of the 'daisy of death.'

Many in the new age spiritual community are people who have outgrown the man-made God of yore. They may see God as a woman or Goddess, an aspect of nature, or a tribunal of higher beings that serve humanity. It really isn't important how you conceptualize Source. It only matters that it is truly based on love and not on old conditioning.

Unfortunately, a lot of the practices in the new age spiritual space are still representative of what we all experienced in a man-made God reality. Anything that is considered a 'must' behavior is programming of some kind from past eras. When people outgrow the conventional man-made God but are still caught up in the group mentality of spirituality, they are still operating under the control of the ego. This stagnant state is referred to being trapped in the daisy of death.

The daisy of death is an energetic mechanism that literally prevents the soul from transcending to the pure positive realms beyond the mind. It is depicted in the spiritual circles as a drawing called the 'flower of life.' People use it to depict their spirituality. But they are really depicting the daisy of death.

The true flower of life is a drawing that has more geometric touch points in it than the daisy of death. The daisy of death looks two dimensional. It is based on a series of points using the number 6. But the true flower of life has more points in it and is three dimensional in nature. It is depicted as fluid energy where at any one point, the energy of one flower of life, can flow into the energy of another flower of life in a movement like an infinity symbol.

Jen sees the daisy of death as an energetic forcefield that prevents souls from moving freely into the higher realms. This force field is a natural barrier caused by the ego energy of opinions, absolutes, unchallenged beliefs, and a strong sense of self. Outmoded spiritual practices – even within the new age spirituality space – hold people in the grips of the daisy of death.

The structure of the daisy of death is made by concepts that we just don't challenge. For most people, linear time is an absolute concept that they are hell-bent on adhering to in this world. So, time would be a lattice structure that is put in place to keep you in the mental realms and prevent you from accessing the higher worlds.

Everything you believe as an absolute becomes another lattice holding you in the grip of the daisy of death. It could be spiritual beliefs, attachments to certain things, and different aspects of life that you rely on as reference points in this world.

When people go through enlightenment, they may feel insane because all the lattices of this world are removed for a short time so they can experience themselves beyond the realms of the ego. As freeing and as exhilarating as this is, the mind may process this as insanity at first. It is okay to relax and realize that you are safe and loved through all your experiences.

In preparing to write this chapter introduction, I asked Jen to provide some practical advice that people can follow to help them live a spiritual life beyond the concept of a man-made God. Here is her list of top tips:

- Do not take ownership of issues or situations that you don't want to own. Think of issues in a detached way.

Saying 'my' when referring to an issue or an ailment is like gluing it to your energy system.

- Challenge any ideas or beliefs that you hold as absolute truths. There is always a more expansive way to look at any situation.

- Practice easily changing your vantage point by seeing the same interaction from different points of view, including that of inanimate beings around you.

- Pay attention to your words. Every word has a vibration to it. Choose your words as carefully as you choose fresh fruit. Pay attention to certain words that make you feel good inside. Say more of them. Notice how some words create a heaviness inside. Use less of them.

- Edit your thoughts to only give energy to those things that you want to manifest for yourself. Indulging in negative thoughts about yourself is self-defeating. Having a poor image of yourself is the ego being just as out of balance as someone who is a braggart. It's just an example of the door swinging the other way.

- You don't need to be superior in every way. All individuals of the collective are an aspect of your own self. This understanding allows you to be much more gracious with other people. Nurturing this understanding can create a more cohesive humanity.

- World peace has been depicted as a form of socialism. This has caused people to reject the possibility of it. World peace does not create the apathy of socialism. World peace is everyone serving humanity through sharing their gifts. This joy alone keeps people too busy to care about judging or subjugating others.

- Thinking you don't have abundance is as silly as thinking that the sun shines for everyone but you.

- No one can destroy you from the outside. They can merely talk you into destroying yourself. So, don't let them.

- Talking about the past is a way of taking dead energy and inserting it into the sacred moment. It is a form of bringing back an experience that should already be resolved.

- Talking about the future before it is manifested is a way of locking one into a limited trajectory from a less informed vantage point.

- Talking about a project before it is completed wastes the energy allotted to finishing it. You can finish a project, or you can talk about a project. It is your choice.

- Gratitude is a means of opening your energy system to receive more abundance. Regret and fear are pathways to closing your energy system to receiving abundance.

- When you are feeling vulnerable, see it as a blow to the ego and allow the ego to take the hits. This will loosen its grip of control on you.

- If someone is angry with you, allow them to deplete all the hate on you as a target. Don't volley the anger back to them. Doing that will just further fuel their rage.

- Whenever there is an absolute in your life, challenge the limitation it puts on you. Usually there is an ancestral imprint or social programming in place.

- When you hear something that is jarring, get a sense of who might benefit from you believing that vantage point.

- Everything you have ever experienced is represented in your present life. You can get a sense of yourself as an eternal being from your ability or capacity to love.

- The mind has limitations whereas the heart has no boundaries. If you want to advance beyond your human conditioning, operate from the heart instead of the mind.
- Expressing creativity in any form is a means of stretching your consciousness and touching others in energy.
- The purpose of all forms of artistic creativity is to inspire creativity in the receiver.

It is not easy to live a spiritual life. I trust that the insights, poems and artwork in this chapter will assist you to live your best life.

Marvin Schneider
Wodonga, Australia
March 2022

Angel's Hue

Stretch your arms into the sky
Pluck out the farthest star
Display it on your bedpost
To remember who you are.

Dig with earnest into the earth
Find the deepest root
Remind yourself from where you come
Mark it with your boot.

Delve into the pain you covet
And have sheltered from your tears
Break the schism of separation
This world is a house of mirrors.

Question all that matters
Everything you've known since birth
Discard all layers of conditioning
That have rusted upon your worth.

Reawaken the aspect of your sweet self
That knows you as being the best
Unshackle all the bad memories from your skin
They were merely a spiritual test.

You are the Light rooted in earth
The rest is the house of illusion
Shatter the mirrors, stop believing the lies
Let go of the pain and confusion.

Reclaim your spirit! Realize your worth!
You were merely asleep, so awaken
Emanate joy, realize love
Remember the dream you've forsaken.

You are abundance, so cash yourself in
You are the gain that you seek
A course of miracles in your own book of life
Just open you up, take a peek.

You are a windfall, you are your own church
You are a prayer, so just say you
A brush stroke of truth swept across the night sky
An individual angel's hue.

Turning Point

In the darkest part of night
When apathy is at its crest
Those immersed in selfish hate
Are clearly at their best.

The tides of life have boiled and churned
Creating a nasty brew
Those slowly enslaved through centuries
Didn't know what to do.

The fate of Earth was waning down
An exacerbated greed
Nothing could save the world
But pure nectar from love's mead.

In this coarse vibration
Bastions of angels volunteered
To incarnate unknowingly
The mission commandeered.

The odds were stacked against them
Success was a shot in the dark
They couldn't know through human eyes
The turning point they marked.

One came upon the horizon
Invisible to most
Who sensed through her physical self
The healing she would host.

Through a desperate need to give
She befriended the Adepts
Listened to their plan for Earth
While everyone else just slept.

Hungry egos were inflated
They couldn't help themselves
They shut down higher senses
Put them all on shelves.

The simplest task could be complete
Only if forming a line
How could the message get to them
That they were in fact divine.

She listened to the Adepts
Created a morse code
For the angelic being in us all
Could know in human mode.

She fought the greatest factions
Who wanted her to fail
They were hell bent against the notion
That humanity would prevail.

The SFT tapping
Is humanity's greatest tool
To pierce through all embedded pain
Dissolve intentions to be cruel.

As more adopt the freedom
That SFT tapping is for
Awakening is as simple as turning on a light
And walking through a door.

The Wayshower

Love is my religion
Joy is my decree
Where I stand is where I worship
My altar is just me.

Kindness is my donation
Giving is my prayer
I don't send it to the sky
I send it everywhere.

Empowering others is my conviction
Needing nothing is my strength
Inspiration is the Wayshower
To which I have at length.

My halo is invisible
My wings are folded in
I'd rather show others their own virtue
Than threaten them with sin.

Seeing good in all others
Is the constant flame I stoke
I prefer to bless them with my words
Than regret a thing I spoke.

I command the heavens
To part the clouds of night
So all can know their windfall
In sound, in love and light.

Join me on this journey
To the worlds of calm, so still
Where everyone is empowered
And centered in free will.

There is no more point in taking
From a spiritual vantage you'll see
That by truly giving heart, mind, and soul
You have an express pass to be free.

Love Is All You Are

A thousand feet away
Is all the joy you need
Take that one short journey
You deserve it in Godspeed.

A hundred feet away
Is all the love you can endure
It is your own base nature
Because your heart is pure.

Twenty feet away
Perhaps it's hard to believe
Is the abundance of all riches
Just be ready to receive.

A few short steps away
Freedom is in your grasp
Have you the nerve to take it
Do you even have to ask?

Step into your center
Why did it take so long
Joy, love, abundance is your birthright
Freedom is your song.

Take off the garbs of illusion
Matter, energy, time, and space
You are oh so everything
You centered is a loving place.

Reunite with all the wonder
Collect love on you like the dew
It's magnetically attracted to
Everything you think, feel, say, and do.

Feel love in your atoms
Pulsing through your very veins
Love is all you see, hear, and feel
And everything that remains.

Sense the importance of the journey
In the lifespan of every soul
To realize we are immersed in love
And being love is the only goal.

We are actually always love
Being the opposite is the illusion
Thinking we are separated
Is what creates all the confusion.

But when you listen to your heart
Ignoring endless mind resolve
Love will be your everything
So let everything else dissolve.

When?

If not peace......What?
If not now......When?
If not to uplift......Why?
If not with love......How?
If not here......Where?
If not you......Who?

Truth

Truth is not won by drawing a line in the sand
It's etched in the heart what the mind can't withstand.

It's forged in a brow all too familiar with pain
Yet too filled with resolve to hold onto disdain.

It's not built up in columns or a heavy façade
It follows along the cracks of each meandering Le Maurade.

It bleeds through the fibers of the ego's tattered remains
'Til all is bleached unrecognizable but the humility stains.

It crumbles the vestige of the smallness of Man
Reunites the omega with the alpha, where individuals began.

Within You

If someone...

Tells you to be quiet
It means you have something to say
Tells you to work
Respond by going to play.

Says that you're ugly
They're missing your beauty within
Tells you you're bad
They are caught up in sin.

Lies to your face
They are really lying to themselves
Tells you how to behave
They have put freedom on a shelf.

Perceives you as poor
They are demonstrating lack
Believes they are owed
It's proves they're not giving back.

Everything others convey
Is the depth of their own truth
Some stay in shallow waters
Well past their youth.

It is you who needs to dismiss
Everything you think, say, or do
The only voice that matters
Is the one within you.

Love's Compassion

Hate saw Love and was enraged
Love saw Hate and felt compassion
Hate shook its fist at Love
Love kept its distance out of deference
Hate attacked Love but lost its balance and fell
Love kept its composure
Hate cried
Love answered its call
Love helped Hate up
Hate looked at Love and was confused
Hate thought that it was Love
Hate now knew what Love looked like
Hate melted into Love at the realization
Love collected itself and went on its way.

Where Truth and Love Began

Speak in the language of the Gods
Unencumbered by the tongue
Dance your virile empowerment
A bastion of the young.

Detach the talons of time and space
From the countenance of You
Shatter all disfiguring misnomers
From all you think, say, feel, or do.

Streamline your outer vision
All but kindness disallow
There's no need to ask questions
Your true self knows the How.

Debunk all the illusion
Of the pettiness of life
Divorce want, need, greed, and power
Take contentment as your wife.

Do these things to heal the wounds
Inflicted through the pettiness of Man
Your journey is always in the moment
Where truth and love began.

The Celebration

Anger took one look around
He had his reasons, they all were sound.

For every outcry and display
Every injustice he did relay.

The price he paid was all too dear
The kingdom was too numb to hear.

Indifference was just in this same stance
But now it was Anger with the ugly glance.

Pride and Arrogance were forlorn
For it was Anger from which they're born.

Hate stood burning their heritage
As Love knitted together a solid bridge

Arrogance took one last look around
He dropped his tilted ugly crown.

Pride dramatically fell to his knees
Tossed Grace and Kindness the palace keys.

There was a different sort of dance
Once Grace and Kindness could relax.

No longer twisted in a spire
The guests could now rise above the mire.

Joy, Love, Abundance inwardly crept
From the chambers where they wept.

As they were seated back where they belong
The celebration erupted in song.

If you were there, you'd know the score
Pride and Vanity are no more.

Truth and Integrity have regained its reign
In the heart of Humanity it will remain.

An Easy Sell

The Golden Amber of an azure sky
Erases the memory of times gone by.

Turn off the news, sit within
Forget all talk of war and sin.

Your heart is a working aperture, a dial
You can open it in nature or with a smile.

It's set closed by all the pain you endure
But it needs to be open for your love to be pure.

We need to accept the depth of who we all are
Forgo every transgression or being transfixed on a scar.

The collective of all needs to undo that dial
Unjar the crust, sit with themselves for a while.

See the azure sky as more than fodder for art
But the beckoning within to a luminous heart.

Not just for us or we'd stay wallowing in pride
For all souls who call earth the home they reside.

When turning the dial, let the worry rescind
Then love in this world will collectively begin.

You can witness the news till you're blue in the face
But it won't heal the world like a pure act of grace.

You can beat both your fists until they're bruised, battered, and broken
But it won't be as powerful as when truth is spoken.

You can deny all you want through a shit-eating grin
But it won't heal that abused inner child within.

Be one of the awakening unfurling your wings
Experience the empowerment that kindness brings.

Then all outer circumstances will flip on a dime
Wonder will bloom, inner music will chime.

Then everyone everywhere may start to agree
In this powerful intention for the collective We.

Maybe you'll feel love not just for those that you bore
But for every single stranger on the way to the store.

And as pure love pumps out from that perpetual old well
The concept of truth, love, and kindness will be easy to sell.

You Exponentially

Energy doesn't flow
Up and down
It churns everywhere
All around.

You don't need to get
From here to there
You exist
Everywhere.

You don't need to juggle
Things to do
Just stand in your center
They will rotate to you.

We don't march through life
Soldiers of time
We are children of the universe
The new paradigm.

We are expressive, creative
Dynamic and free
We are everything to everyone
We imagine ourselves to be.

We live beyond the concepts
Of birth, pain, or death
We are as free as a windfall
Expansive as breadth.

Open your horizons
To all that you are
Not a pile of flesh
But a perpetual star.

Blazing in glory
Beyond even the sky
Stop wondering WHO you are
And start asking Why?

Like why are you determined
To play it so small
Why don't you dance in the heavens
Heed the ethereal call?

Why not realize yourself
Exponential and free?
This is the You
You came here to be.

Book of Life

Pay deference to things you fear
That have captured your attention
They have put a face upon
What's too hideous to mention.

Past life memories buried deep
Incest, torture, murder, rage
They are teachers perhaps mentors
Dog-eared chapters in your page.

Insert your story amongst the others
A wealth of wisdom gleaned from strife
Use your love as the glue
To secure yourself in the Book of Life.

Sing

Hold a steady course
Don't give in to the mind
Not seeing the solution
Doesn't make you blind.

Feel life with your heart
Deep into your soul
Being kind, joyful, and free
Is the ultimate goal.

You can't get there in theory
Or on the backs of the crowd
It comes through discerning truth
And voicing it aloud.

Delve into the trenches
Hide there if you choose
Love and truth are your mainstay
They are something you can't lose.

It doesn't matter how you distract
From your ultimate goal
No matter what you believe
You're still loving and whole.

Look up from your drudgery
The one in which you cling
You were not meant to suffer
You were meant to sing.

Discernment

I don't make a habit of asking for help
But will give it when it's truly needed
I know the difference between the truth and a lie
And how easily ill will is seeded.

I understand all that ever transpires
Will be up for debate or discussion
But I tune out all the mental fray
Just like any form of annoying percussion.

I don't ever fixate on a problem
Never give attention to an unworthy cause
I never listen to whiny complaints
Unless the disgruntled has paws.

Kindness is a form of palpable truth
That can be felt by the discerning eye
It registers itself on all planes of existence
And encourages us to give it a try.

We, together, are all palpable truth
Connected by a lattice of love
We are all agents of truth learning to thrive
As below, to reflect above.

Love's Appeal

Tell me I don't matter
Tell me you don't care
Tell me it's all bullshit
That you're not really there.

Tell me there's no freedom
That everything's a lie
Carelessly chuckle and walk away
As you watch me die.

Or...

Tell me there is purpose
In all we say and do
Give me reason to believe
In love, in life, in you.

Plant a garden with your words
Make each day a song
Give all a reason to hope
Tell us we belong.

Give all purpose, don all truths
Make all scenarios win/win
From the ashes of defeat
Sprouts of providence begin.

See peace when others envision war
Talk advantage when others spout loss
Risk vulnerability and feeling raw
Show kindness at all cost.

Encourage, enlighten, visualize, evolve
Empathize, appreciate, heal
Cater to one's sense of higher self
To deliver love's appeal.

It doesn't really matter
What you say or do
As long as you act from the depth of love
And know that place is you.

We Can

My job as a human is simply to Be
Convert every experience in relationship to me
I'm every windfall, I'm every dream
I'm every ocean, I'm every stream.

I'm every adventure that could happen to Man
I live with intention, I do what I can
I know this capacity shrinks when I fear
It goes totally dormant when I show I don't care.

Indifference allows others to prey on my zeal
To take potential from all, they cheat, lie and steal
So instead of being everything that floats on the breeze
They become the apocalypse, they become the disease.

They stand on the sidelines, roped in by fear
Too proud to speak or show that they care
They give away their power to all who walk by
The dictates of society say not to ask why.

War, depression, and disease have become the norm
Cannabis and Xanax, the only port in the storm
People are broken and wore down to the soul
To be left alone is their last standing goal.

Change can happen if the collective of Man
Steps up to the plate and says that we can
We can change the world together, let's give it a try
Lets show kindness to all instead of just walking by.

Let's remember our dreams, express them out loud
Voice aspiration, send it off in a cloud
Withdraw our agreement in the destruction of Man
We are creating a shift simply by saying, 'We can.'

We can return to our most heartfelt desire
To live with integrity, contribute, inspire
We can return to the wonderment that can set us all free
We are every potential, we are every tree.

When you give love to you, it's bestowed upon me
We are all in this together, joyful, loving and free
We are the windfall happening to Man
In this very moment by declaring, 'We can.'

Celebrating the Moment of Now

Raise a chalice to your lips
Taste the nectar of love's bliss
Celebrate in the light of the fire within
Dance to the rhythm of love.

Whistle a lover's tune in your heart
Where the milk of experience wells
Take a warrior's view and a lover's stance
In the cause of the moment of now.

Dreams of worlds basted in gold
Remembered promises kissed with a vow
And secrets unabashedly shared
Are contained in each moment of love.

Gain footing on the step you already took
Reach for the branch you're already on
Turn around if you can and look at yourself
Your journey is in the moment of now.

Integrity's Blueprint

Give more than you get
Reap less than you sow
Listen more than you speak
Realize more than you know.

Calm much more than agitate
Question more than comply
Hold yourself to higher standards
Extinguish every lie.

Dream bigger than attainable
Realize your own worth
Create thoughts of originality
Celebrate every birth.

Lead when there needs leadership
Follow when it seems best
Acknowledge greatness in us all
Ignore everything that's left.

Have a higher calling
Know a greater truth
Have the wisdom of experience
Flexibility of youth.

Cheer the world to victory
If only in your mind
Make changes you envision
Forgive those running blind.

Follow your inner compass
Do everything you can
To uplift the course of humanity
By loving the heart of man.

Love's Final Decree

Wait out the pain
It does have an end
Like looking up at the clouds
For the rain to descend.

Let it drip through your hair
And fall upon the ground
As the force of the break
Reverberates and resounds.

Crack open the nut
Where the anguish was held
Pull out the shriveled meat
That caused you such dread.

Recover your composure
From that punch in the gut
No, you aren't shattered
You're still the whole nut.

Recover your dignity
Walk away clean
You are guided in all endeavors
By forces unseen.

Refute the notion
That you go it alone
You are honored as sacred
There's no sin to atone.

Let the silence and loneliness
Cut through the façade
Rip through layers of bullshit
As the angels applaud.

What you hold dear
As your own private hell
Drives you to hear truth
As clear as a bell.

As truth now personified
To this we agree
To hold space in this world
For love's final decree.

Bless This Day

Bless this day
And those I serve
May all know the truth
They so richly deserve.

May all open their hearts
Their souls, and their minds
Give others the fortitude
To truly be kind.

May all open their awareness
So they can happily refrain
From abusing others
And bringing disdain.

Give all the insight
So they can all see
Everyone beautifully abundant
Loving and free.

Integrity's By-Laws

Heaven is won by the blessings we share
Hell is defined when we don't seem to care
Let's work to upgrade our set of by-laws
By pointing out strengths instead of the flaws.

How we treat others
Is our personalized cadence
A unique brand of kindness
Our own providence.

In a world that is steeped in the depth of illusion
And those who see truth are diagnosed with delusion
They fall through the cracks into society's bad grace
Reality is the egg on conformity's face.

We call forth and honor
Those of integrity's creed
They hold a higher vibration
Mass enlightenment's seed.

Cast away the demons
That leave us deaf, mute, and blind
Return to the love
Leave all transgressions behind.

Burst open your heart
Pull out all reserve
Rewrite the by-laws
Of what we deserve.

The Depth of You

Dissolve all trepid inclinations
Spritz them in the wind
Empty out your fibers
Until pain and angst rescind.

Untangle every twine of worry
Like finely braided hair
Comb them out from root to shaft
Until you just don't care.

Breathe a new sense of wonder
Into every aspect of your home
Instead of settling complacently
Permit yourself to roam.

Set out on an adventure
With everything you do
Jump the fence and blur all lines
Between love and life and you.

Mingle with the salt of the Earth
Dine at the hearth of all
Sip sweetly on a wine of contentment
Break through every possible wall.

Dance in wild abandonment
All the rest of your days
Realize there is no end
Seer through finality's haze

Rest sweetly in the confidence
Of all the good you do
Then take a breath, perhaps a pause
To honor the depth of you.

CHAPTER 9

Inspiration

THE OVERWHELMING impression I get from having watched hundreds of Jen's recorded private sessions with clients, is that many people who are already on a spiritual journey are finding it tough going. I often wonder how people who are not on a spiritual path are coping. The purpose of this chapter, and indeed the entire book, is to give the reader context, hope and inspiration when traversing the seemingly chaotic dynamics of life.

It is useful to explore the question as to why so many people are finding it difficult to make sense of life these days. I am sure there are plenty of 'this world' contributing factors, including the pressure of the 24-hour news cycle, the impact of social media, the polarization of society, the increasing wealth gap, and the pressures and expectations that society puts on us in terms of careers, property ownership and family life. But I would like to explore this issue from a broader perspective.

There are two main things from a broader perspective that I believe are contributing to the difficulties that a lot of people are facing when navigating through life. The first is the accelerated need to clear stagnant energy and engrams of past-life trauma to transcend the ego as part of the ascension process. The second is the increasing influence of intangible stimuli that a lot of people are struggling to process. It is the increasing and accelerated nature of these things that I think is causing a lot of people difficulty.

There is a real imperative to go through the ascension process at this time in Earth's evolution. Ascension is the process of transcending the ego. And as entrenched as it is, the ego is a fragile thing. It can be easily wounded. Confronting the ego can be a very painful process which brings forward emotions of anger, fear, loneliness, shame and regret. Little wonder then that a lot of people are bringing up painful emotions as we accelerate in the mass ascension process. Most people spend a lot of energy suppressing these emotions.

It is equally important to recognize that a lot of people are now beginning to experience energetic stimuli that they may not yet know how to process. These can come in the form of images, sounds, voices, or feelings. Having these new experiences 'out of the blue' can be very frightening and confusing. It could leave you feeling as if you are possessed or going insane. I have watched several private session recordings where Jen helped the client navigate through these senses.

It is interesting to observe that a lot of people on the spiritual path are actively seeking to awaken their kundalini, receive shaktipat from a guru, or open their third eye. Jen has said several times that such instantaneous activations of energy, while exhilarating at the time, can be very challenging for a lot of people to process. I get the sense that Jen thinks it is preferrable to learn to walk before you run.

Thankfully, Jen offers some advice for people to help them navigate through these seemingly chaotic dynamics of life.

It is useful to understand that this is all part of the ascension process. It is formula. So simply having an awareness of what is going on will help allay a sense of isolation, confusion, and thinking you are losing your mind. You are not. We are all aspects of Source having a human experience for the purpose of expanding universal consciousness on the pathway to ascension. Perhaps it is easier to detach yourself from the current experience when you think about them in the broader perspective of evolving through a myriad of lifetimes. As difficult as it is in the moment, it is useful to look at situations and experiences from a detached or neutral position without labelling or judging them as either good or bad.

A very practical thing you can do is to identify the experience or emotion as it is happening and run through the SFT tapping protocols to address it. Those protocols, and how to use them, are provided in Jen's book *The SFT Lexicon: Second Edition* available from the Jenuine Healing website.

And of course, we all need a little bit of upliftment, encouragement, and inspiration from time to time. So, may the poems and artwork in this chapter give you the inspiration you need when the going gets tough.

Marvin Schneider
Wodonga, Australia
March 2022

Encouragement

They said you'd never amount to much
They said your dreams were out of touch
They said the You you want to be
Doesn't quite fit in society.

They said the pain and wounded pride
Will help you take it all in stride
It's okay to have a broken heart
Just don't let them see you fall apart.

But, you ask,
Isn't it better if I try?
No! You'll achieve success
When you see pigs fly.

Well, there's something you need to know
Dreams, like seeds, are meant to grow
When they are put in the ground
It's only to spread their bloom around.

Every dream that's deprived of air
Possibility hears, 'I don't care'
Every hope that wanders in the woods
Was led astray by a trail of Shoulds.

For every forsaken potential crying
There's a wistful grounded winged pig sighing
Some may stand by and watch dreams die
But I'll be coaching pigs to fly.

What Would Dr. Seuss Say?

You think I'm here
And you are there
But you are here
Here is there.

We are here
Here is now
We are in
The Here and Now.

You think I'm great
And you are small
That makes no sense
No sense at all.

How can it be when I am you
We are the same
Just one
Not two?

As a fact
We are all one
It's always been
Since life begun.

We are not separate
You and me
We are the same
We are the We.

The world is made of
One big We
We span the globe
This We that's me.

When you are hurt
We feel the same
We cry and shout
And give out blame.

We defend ourselves
Exhaust our wits
Stomp about
In angry fits.

But when we perch
To strike a blow
Then is the time
We need to know.

When we hurt them
We hurt the We
I hurt you
You hurt me.

Let's turn the tables
On this game
Disarm the drones
And refrain.

When you want
To hate yourself
See me crying
On a shelf.

When you want
To say you're bad
Realize
You've just been had.

The hate you give
To your Me
Is the plight of
The universal We.

If you want to
Heal the All
Crumble that
Inner wall.

The wall that says
We can't all be
Wonderfully abundant
Happy, free.

One Little Human

One little human
Falling away from the pack
Can restore hope to the world
Bring humanity back.

One little human
Stepping away from the crowd
Can feel the anguish of the multitudes
And voice it out loud.

One little human
Scarred and nearly broken
Can take joy, truth, and love
Where it's never been spoken.

One little human
Abiding by love's creed
Can heal the whole world
Let's wish it Godspeed.

One little human
It may very well be you
Can show all other humans
What they are able to do.

One Little Human: The Dichotomy

One little human
Pathetic and small
Is deaf, mute, and blind
To humanity's call.

One little human
Shrouded in greed
Refuses the cries
That the innocent plead.

Possessed with a notion
At insanity's crest
That his actions are justified
His genocide blessed.

One little human
A face in the crowd
Can personify cruelty
Command it out loud.

Etched in the heavens
Is the hell one man inflicts
Through the horror of war
That Ukrainian rubble depicts.

One little human
Be grateful it's not you
Is the face of evil intentions
And the damage they do.

Yet

When you have given everything you can
But still go another round
When you've had the snot kicked out of you
Yet stand and hold your ground.

When your wings have been crushed
For who knows why
Yet you design your own flight path
And find a way to fly.

When you are totally dismissed
And left without a voice
But still advocate for others
Because you simply have no choice.

When everyone seems to lie
Denying their highest truth
Yet you hold all accountable
From world leaders to the youth.

When your heart has been a battlefield
A perpetual push turns to shove
Yet you manage to transcend it all
And find a way to love.

When you pour yourself into life
With nothing else to give
Then you have found the answer to the question
What's the proper way to live?

Homage to You

You are as fluid as an ocean
More expansive than the sky
As determined as an echo
More breathless than a sigh.

Astonishing as a pipe dream
That has met its manifestation
As pure as the sanctity of a soul
Reaching its final destination.

You are a joyful whisper
Completed in a smile
The perfect pair of running shoes
That can go the extra mile.

You are divinity personified
That leaves no second guess
Where the alpha and omega meet
Is you, humanly expressed.

Loved on All Sides

You don't need an agenda
You don't need a cause
You don't need a platform
To draw in applause.

You don't need to be seen
You don't need to be heard
You don't need to do anything
That belief is absurd.

You don't need to prove anything
To show what you're worth
You've been loved beyond measure
Eons before your last birth.

You are cradled in acceptance
Nestled in love
It may not feel so from below
But you're complete from above.

You are cheered on by angels
Mentored by guides
Accepted unconditionally
Loved on all sides.

The Miracle of You

Kindness is my prayer
Encouragement is my song
Sincerity is my anthem
Singing it makes me strong.

Connectedness is my motto
Service is my decree
Helping others is my virtue
Doing so sets me free.

Taking is sometimes giving
Receiving graciously is a gift
Justice is spontaneous
The law of love works swift.

Everything you think
Everything you do
Is meant to excel you further
Into the miracle of you.

If denial is your option
Ignorance is it too
Intelligence isn't awareness
That's what smart people misconstrue.

Awareness leads from the heart
Intelligence may follow
A good mind without the heart
Can leave one feeling hollow.

But a heart with pure intention
Has warmth and depth to spare
That is how they're recognized
They have ample love to share.

What You Are Capable Of

Can you be someone's guardian angel
Give from an infinite source?
Can you guide them back on track
When they veer off course?

Can you be a champion
Of light, and love, and truth?
Can you inspire the very old
Temper the foolishness of youth?

Can you wrap your love around
The mute, the deaf, the blind?
Can you help them speak and hear
And see the world as kind?

Can you teach the selfish
What satisfaction it is to give?
Can you stir passion in the disheartened
Imbue a joyful will to live?

Can you teach a random stranger
The philosophy of a tree?
Can you help them heart, mind, and soul
Be completely free?

Can you gather all your courage
To be loving to the core?
This is what you're capable of
All this, and so much more!

Beauty

There's no need to travel to where beauty dwells
It springs abundantly from an infinite well
Not a place that one needs to see
More of a constant reminder to learn, to just Be.

Open the doorway to stillness, walk inside
Grasp spiritual laws and easily abide
See your inner light so crystal, so clear
Know your own emanation diffuses all fear.

Walk the edge between consciousness and fate
Defy limitations at an alarming rate
Finally seeing what was already there
The wonderment of nature that you bear.

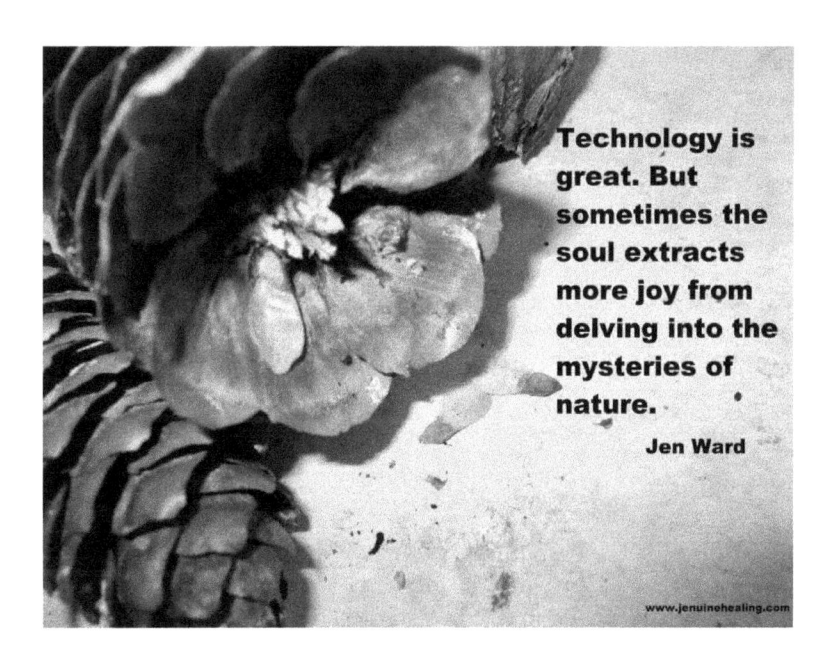

> **Technology is great. But sometimes the soul extracts more joy from delving into the mysteries of nature.**
>
> **Jen Ward**

Live Life Boldly!

Gazelles don't go down without a fight
Stars don't just hover in the night
Dreams aren't dreamt to be suspended
Live life boldly!
As intended.

True Abundance

Pierce the sheath of indifference
With the angst of an expectant heart
Live way beyond all your means
You've carried true wealth from the start.

Brush the strands from your vision
Wipe sweat from the furrowed brow
Tilt your visor to change its angle
See your abundance here and now.

Dance in her ample presence
Taste her saltiness on your skin
You have always known her secret
Her true riches lie within.

Embrace your stately purpose
Recognize providence beyond all wealth
Abundance is the robe you walk in
Wear it always in good health.

True Strength

All the times I was misunderstood
Taught me the patience to know
That when I am feeling confused and alone
Is when I'm most ready to grow.

All the times that I have cried
Showed me joy in letting tears flow
All those who took pleasure in deceiving me
Gave me the conviction to trust what I know.

All the times I have been lonely
Taught me the language of the trees
Being constantly told what to do
Taught me to do just as I please.

I'm grateful for being shown ugliness
I see beauty now everywhere
Without a trace of a competitive edge
I see life as always too fair.

Thank you for showing me cruelty
So that I can see others in pain
It's not me that they want to suffer
They lash out in pure self-disdain.

Thank you for each lesson
Where I receive just enough
I'm not distracted by want and need
Or buried in lots of stuff.

Thank you for the capacity to love
That I nurture at great length
Perhaps I heal through this intention
Everything else merely gives me strength.

One Ancient Celestial Tune

If someone tells you a lie
Use it to discern truth
If they proclaim that you are old
Be determined to keep your youth.

If someone tells you that you're ugly
Show the world how beautiful you are
If they discredit your life's battle
Don't hesitate to show them the scar.

If someone tells you you're wrong
Keep the conviction that you are right
When they relentlessly discourage
Keep your true objective in sight.

If someone stomps on your dreams
Breathe life into them with your wonder
Don't try to convert them to your truth
Forgo that pressure you're under.

If someone tries to discredit you
Let your integrity refute their claim
Let silence purge all the pettiness
Then only the calm will remain.

If someone tries to deflate you
Hunker down and just say, 'No'
You can only be led astray
To the point you're willing to go.

If someone asks something in sincerity
Demonstrate how much you care
They have been conditioned as you have
To believe true compassion is rare.

If someone tries to stroke your ego
Brush off their gross offense
You do not fall for flattery
Never ever feed off such pretense.

Show them how to greet you
In the neutrality of love's breath
This is the way to convince them
Of the magnitude of their own depth.

Emanate from deep within
Reflect their light back onto them
From the flowering of this gesture
Blossoms of world peace will stem.

Whisper their greatness into their heart
With the resonance of pure song
They then will remember their true nature
Realizing it was them all along.

Lead them into the forever of the moment
As a form of an ancient decree
Through this act of altruism
They can know what it's like to be free.

They will now see their place here as timeless
Emanating with the stars and the moon
Knowing we all make up the collective
As one ancient celestial tune.

The Troubadour

Here he is to settle
A soul's old score
In the humble garb
Of a Troubadour.

Fanning the flame
Of the passion of youth
Into all worlds
With melodic truth.

The hero and zealot
Have nothing on him
Song is his ocean
Sink, float, or swim.

Selflessness exudes
Every last pore
In living his purpose
He suffers no more.

Speaking the ancient
Language of love
He administers truth
To below as above.

With no ill intention
To capture the praise
Love's floodgates are opened
Lock levels are raised.

Let no more folly
Be wasted in speed
The virtue of the song
Is his own special mead.

CHAPTER 10

Searching for Love

IT SEEMS TO ME that a lot of people are desperately lonely and looking for love. I remember someone asking on one of our early *Jen in her Jammies* podcasts whether we could address the topic of loneliness.[6] Despite all the supposed connections made possible with social media and being surrounded by a mass of people, many people still feel isolated and disconnected from the collective.

The search for love and the topic of loneliness are somewhat interconnected. Those searching for love are likely to fall into one of two camps. The first is that group of people who do not currently have an intimate partner or companion and feel empty and isolated as a result. The second is that group of people who are currently in a relationship, but that relationship is not meeting their expectations or feeding their emotional needs. In either case, the issue involves looking for something they don't have.

The thing that is common between these two groups of people is that they are looking for the resolution of their emptiness in a source that is outside of themselves in the form of another person – mostly an intimate partner. But it

---

[6] You can watch the *Jen in her Jammies* episode on loneliness by typing 'Jenuine Healing Dealing with Loneliness' in the Youtube search bar

is interesting to reflect on the true spiritual nature of love. Love in its true expression is a state of being that is experienced from within through a process of outflowing. It is often the case that when you feel loved by another person, what is really happening is that the other person is holding space for you to feel your own love. What you are really doing is feeling the gratitude and joy of being in close connection with your higher self. And of course, because we are all atoms and an aspect of Source, when we feel a close connection with our higher self, we are really feeling the love of Source.

So, with this understanding, the solution to dealing with loneliness or the search for love is to focus your attention within. You cannot rely on other people or external stimuli to make you happy. Happiness comes from a state of gratitude and contentment within yourself, often derived from a process of outflowing and being of service to others.

The natural state of existence for a spiritual being is to be in a perpetual state of joy, love, abundance, freedom, health, success, security, companionship, creativity, peace, life, wholeness, beauty, enthusiasm, contentment, spirituality, enlightenment, confidence, empowerment, sincerity, integrity, imagination, and kindness. True mastership comes when you are in all of these states at once. So, if you are lacking in one or more of these areas, try to identify the issue causing the lack being experienced, and then do the SFT protocols on that issue.

It is often difficult to identify the issue causing a lack being experienced. After all, if we all knew what the root cause issue is, we would have addressed it by now, right? But nevertheless, the more you can look within and identify root cause issues, the better. Specific root causes to lack are often grounded in past-life engrams that you may not have easy access to. So, it may be helpful to schedule a private session with Jen to help you identify and then remove blockages.

Another option that may be helpful is to take a more generic approach. For example, if you are experiencing a lack of joy in your life, you could do the following SFT tapping sequences:

- the Energetic Cleanse protocol using the phrase '*a lack of joy*' in place of each of the blank spaces;
- the Peanut Butter & Jelly protocol using the word '*me*' in each of the first blank spaces and the phrase '*a lack of joy*' in each of the second blank spaces;
- the Expunging Negativity protocol using the phrase '*a lack of joy*' in place of each of the blank spaces;
- the Positive protocol using the word '*joy*' in each of the blank spaces.

It is difficult to experience the natural states of joy, love, abundance, and so on, while you are still carrying within your energy field past-life traumas and engrams which are holding you hostage in this life. Given you are likely to have had many thousands if not hundreds-of-thousands of lives, it is highly likely that your akashic record will contain the full range of human experiences. So, before tackling joy, love, abundance, and so head on, it would be highly beneficial to first go through the entire series of taps provided in *The SFT Lexicon: Second Edition*.[7] This book contains a comprehensive series of SFT taps addressing over 200 physical, emotional, behavioral and relationship issues.

---

[7] You can order your copy of The SFT Lexicon: Second Edition at https://jenuinehealing.com/product/the-sft-lexicon-second-edition/

True love in a spiritual sense is an inner experience that is often precipitated through outflowing and being of service to others. So, there are two simple but very powerful things you can do in this regard. The first is to do SFT taps to benefit all of humanity. Jen and I regularly run group SFT tapping sessions to free humanity from the clutches of self-interest, power mongers, war, global warming, and other issues facing the human collective and the preservation of the natural environment. The second thing you can do in an outflowing sense is to do SFT taps for your soul mate, wherever they are.

May the poems and artwork in this chapter assist you in your search for inner love.

Marvin Schneider
Wodonga, Australia
March 2022

Search and Rescue

I delve into a pool of quiet conviction
Swim in a sweat soaked sheet of despair
Believe you have left me abandoned
As I reach for you and find nothing there.

Sounds have become tinny and off key
Vision is blurred through the tears
I am dimwitted and dumbfound
To feel that my God doesn't care.

I have fought for you through many lifetimes
Ruthlessly defended your stance
Shamelessly praised you until my voice was left raw
But don't even feel you in any romance.

All of the glorious proclamations
All of the conjecturing from within
All of the pompous genuflecting
Went the way of original sin.

Each kindness is now a sweet victory
Eroding the foolish brash hearted pride
It is by emptying myself of bravado
That I can feel you welling inside.

Now I understand your true nature
It is as pure as a hint of the wind
It is the stillness now that embraces me
Causing all subtle doubt to rescind.

You are the light, the love, and the music
You are the curve of my smile
I searched for you through every disadvantage
You sat with me all of the while.

Now I know how to serve you
By greeting you in all that I meet
No longer is glory my barometer
I have been the victor in every defeat.

Sir, let me walk with you sweetly
Please let me carry your ware
By lightening the load of another
I will always sense God everywhere.

Happiness doesn't come from "having" or "doing"
Happiness comes from "Being"

Jen ward

Being With You

I've searched the heavens to be with you
The depths of hell as well
Dante's Inferno would be a children's book
Compared to the story I tell.

I've ambled through the river Styx
Held rank in the halls of Valhalla
I've searched for you in visions real and sublime
From paradise lost to Shamballa.

I have been anointed by the Valkyrie
Had my head carried away on a stick
Been a vestal virgin to the sacred fire
A sin eater to the dying and sick.

I've lived a thousand hells on earth
Just for the knowing you exist
I've begged the Adepts to intervene for me
Praying for you to walk through the mist.

I have beckoned to you as I lay alone in my bed
Imagined you were there all the while
I never really knew your name
Just your voice, your caress, and your smile.

I've kept my sanity somewhat intact
Through the belief that to you I belong
You are the secret I have perpetually dreamt
Through the apocrypha, the Kali Yuga, a song.

Your love is the main vindication
Being with you is the ultimate high
You are the resolve to every anguish
When I cried in the night simply, 'Why?'

If you want, I will heal the whole planet
If you command, I can purify the Earth
Your love empowers me to heal all life
Simply through validating their worth.

I will uplift all of creation
Release endless suffering too
I am omniscient, and omnipotent Love
Through the sanctity of loving you.

Love's Call

What must I say to inspire you?
What will make you feel more secure?
How can you know the magnitude of your worth
There's reverence for all you endure?

I see all the pain that you carry
All the times you had to go it alone
All the memories you hold of being abandoned
I cried as your heart turned to stone.

I cheered on all your attempts at coping
By focusing on someone to love
How could you know that you've never been lost
Life's guided like the flight of a dove.

Tears are never a cry in the dark
They are a means of flushing out pain
You are learning each moment the depth of your worth
Meeting challenge without hint of disdain.

You've learned you are more than an island
Or a stranger living alone where you dwell
You are an ember in a perpetual blaze
A personified love spark as well.

You carry all the attributes of divinity
Demonstrate them when you're in love
The key is to knowing that love comes from within
Not from without or above.

Glean that special feeling of being in love
Wear it as a second skin
Don't play it safe or the victim
See every scenario as a win-win.

Let love emanate from your very atoms
Have it shine on your face like fresh dew
May it gently whisper in your inner ear
Let it help you recognize it as you.

You hold all the keys to what you pray for
Guard the gate to your own inner realm
You are the master of your divinity
You are the captain at the helm.

Steer yourself always to your own true essence
In your workplace, society, and home
Never again do you need to find love
Never again must you roam.

See love shine in all of nature
From each blade of grass to each tree
Never does it waver from its purpose
Never does it cry out, 'Poor me!'

You are a dance of flawed perfection
An inspiration to one and to all
You are respected beyond all reproach
Simply by heeding love's call.

Stand Still

When was the very first moment
When you suddenly became so scared?
Do you remember the exact instance
You forfeited even trying to care?

When was the actual turning point
You chose to exist rather than thrive?
Did it coincide in any way shape or form
When you stopped appreciating just being alive?

When did you forget to feel
The enthusiasm to be awake?
Was it when you thought someone loved you back
But realized it was just your mistake?

Life and love are messy
We fall, and we collide
We hold on to old resentments
When we feel like we've been denied.

But others are doing the best that they can
Hanging on by their shear will
They never really meant to hurt you
They are not trying to hurt you still.

Love is not the type of thing
That can be taken much for granted
It's not something you need to search for
There's plenty where you're planted.

Stop looking for love as it looks to others
And find what is meant for you
It permeates through everything you are
And everything you do.

Love is the natural byproduct
Of doing what you like best
It's not something that you need to prove
Or win by passing a test.

It's not a narrow expression
Met by just one pair of eyes
It's everyone who enters your day
Whether they crawl, swim, walk, or fly

So here is the secret to receiving love
For the over-zealous mind
Simply forget trying to conquer love
Draw it near just by being kind.

Love will walk right up to you
And easily take you in
It's ready to sweep you off your feet
It isn't something that you need to win.

Love isn't found by hunting it down
Or acquired by sheer will
You will find you are immersed in love
When you finally just stand still.

Loneliness

Embrace loneliness for what it is
Love calling from afar
Depression, angst, and disappointment
False emanations from a star.

For how can light be anything
But beautiful and serene?
Believing you're anything but vibrant and love
Leaves depths of you unseen.

You are amazing as you always will be
There's no point in arguing this truth
You are always as free and expansive
As light, beauty, abundance, and youth.

Step away from the discouragement
The clouds that hide your light
They muddled your mind unintentionally
Hindering the consciousness of your flight.

See truth for what it really is
You are stepping into yourself
Open the door to your own inner worlds
That fear and indifference have put on a shelf.

You are wonderfully awakening
A blossom ready to perch into song
This transient world is not your true home
The heart of love is where you truly belong.

Humanity's Heart

I offer myself up to you love
In a million different ways
As healer, Goddess, woman
My devotion is on display.

My depth is research for your soul
Explore it as you will
I am the chalice that you seek
Drink from me and have your fill.

My heart lies weary at your feet
In longing and unrest
I have waged such battles to be worthy of you
Passed every single test.

I thrive in your kingdom's domain my Love
Banish me no more
By accepting my love back into your life
Its humanity's heart you restore.

Being Invisible

Is there more love and light to give
When beauty fades with its last chagrin
When power plays have come and went
And natural resources have all been spent?

When friends and calls are far between
And contributions go unseen
When all that's left is that one last hope
That there's more beyond the human scope.

The human canvas is camouflage
Not a storage tank for ensilage
Providence happens in a higher place
As love smooths the brow of a weary face.

CHAPTER 11

Finding Love

MANY PEOPLE spend a lot of time and energy looking for the perfect partner in the hope that they will experience love. But they still feel disappointed when they find their perfect partner. So, what does spiritual love feel like?

Jen describes spiritual love as a state of almost nothingness. That makes sense because it reflects a state of perpetual gratitude and contentment. It is beyond the ego.

In a lot of ways, it is when you find spiritual love of this kind that you have achieved spiritual mastery. You are in a perpetual state of joy, love, abundance, freedom, health, success, security, companionship, creativity, peace, life, wholeness, beauty, enthusiasm, contentment, spirituality, enlightenment, confidence, empowerment, sincerity, integrity, imagination, and kindness. At that point, you can stop doing SFT tapping. You are welcome!

Marvin Schneider
Wodonga, Australia
March 2022

One Thought of You

I indulge in one thought of you
Etch it in my mind
It transports me to a providence
That alone I cannot find.

Where love is not counted off in pairs
Single file, two by two
But is lavished generously upon everyone
The multitudes, not the few.

Intimacy is commonplace
Integrity and compassion too
All transactions are transparent
True colors shine right through.

Love is never dormant
Waiting to open just one heart
It is in what we eat, sleep, dream, and do
And of which we're all a part.

It's not cast off with ill regard
Or based upon a whim
No, love is what we walk through
Dance and fly and swim.

One thought of you takes me there
Heals my weary heart
That beats right through the heavy illusion
That we are separate and apart.

Allow me one quick thought of you
That transforms me to a place
Where everyone is immersed in love
In sanctity and grace.

Where love is not contingent
On believing, hope, or prayer
Love is allotted to everyone
And way much easier to share.

Meet me in a land
Devoid of guilt or blame
Where I am allowed to love you
With not one hint of shame.

Meet me at the altar
Where such bliss is meant for only two
But in this altered universe
I give to everyone through you.

I devote my time on earth
To bring others to this world too
This place I can so easily access
With just one thought of you.

jen in her jammies

In Your Eyes

In your presence
I am not lost
You see me
At all cost.

In your bed
I am not used
Humiliated
Ignored, abused.

In your eyes
I'm not demeaned
Invalidated
Or unseen.

In your world
I do exist
Stake a claim
As you insist.

With your tutelage
I am free
To enjoy myself
Discover me.

You are giving
I need not plead
Dismiss myself
Or concede.

In all moments
You make me whole
My better half
You heal my soul.

The Rescue

My feet walked heavy on this Earth
Before you came around
Every experience brought me incredible pain
Every sight, touch, taste, and sound.

Now you've come and raised the veil
Of what this world can reveal
All the beauty, joy, love, and abundance
Is impossible to conceal.

You've lifted me up from a deep despair
Apathy, martyrdom, and defeat
There is now infinite joy in waking up
Every sight, thought, and sound is so sweet.

You are my perpetual Christmas morn
Your smile is in every sunrise
How you have awakened pleasure in me
Is a mystical, magical surprise.

You are every heartfelt promise
I wasn't allowed to entertain
You wipe all the suffering off the planet
Leaving only worldly wonders to remain.

I obediently respect and honor you Love
As Goddess fully centered, complete, and aware
I defer to your council in all possible ways
To demonstrate the amount that I care.

You are my knight in shining armor
Riding into my life on a stead
Striking down all that has afflicted me
Every punishment, rejection, and need.

Sweetly accept all that's offered here Love
To open my heart even more
Walk through the chambers of my inner prison
Unlock that one last vested door.

Whisper nice things in my energy Love
Coo sweetly as you coax me to sleep
Be patient as I extract every last tear
Hold me tight to your chest as I weep.

Let me relax in your arms once again
For the first time in a few centuries
Let's bask in the promise that our union reveals
In the stillness, the stars, and the breeze.

The Worthiest Goal

Every thought of you is sacred
Your kisses, heaven's wine
Loving you is a Godsend
Your presence is my shrine.

Living without you is a sepulcher
I've cast myself in since youth
Knowing you only in energy
Has been life's painful truth.

I've hardly survived without you Love
Subsisting on a wing and a prayer
Lamenting in the darkness
For not finding you anywhere.

You finally stepped out of the mist
After I had giving up all hope
When life was a losing lottery game
Leaving no more reasons to cope.

But now every moment is exponential joy
Filled with embellishments of you
My heart is an open window
As desire for you flows through.

You fill me like a chalice
That's spilling over at the brim
Call on me to pleasure you
I'll satiate every whim.

You now are my only prayer book Love
I'm yours mind, body, and soul
To please you in all moments and realms
Is my worthiest of goals.

Why?

I've stripped off all my layers for you
I stand before you bare
Exposed my vulnerability in gooseflesh
To show you how much I care.

I can see all your wounds too Love
The ones you try to hide
I unzip you like a jacket
Gently slip myself inside.

I heal your worries from within
Remove daggers from your back
May my skills in tending all your needs
Excuse the female prowess that I lack.

How many ways can we complete each other
Without the other one drowning?
Our coos of virtuoso in the night
Voice humanity's love resounding.

Tend me like a fire my Love
Lay your body near
With each lick of my flame
I prove how much I care.

Gaze on me like the ocean Love
Covet me like the sky
May you never doubt how much you're loved
May you never question, 'Why?'

Ducks in a Row

To writhe in pleasure as we awake
To sing your praises for your own sake
To give you all the credit that you're due
To live each moment entwined with you.

To feel your presence in every dawn
Knowing for certain all demons are gone
To sidestep the past without even a care
Hope springs eternal knowing you're here.

The whispered secrets, I've kept in my heart
Sharing them eagerly, right from the start
To have nothing to run from, nothing to hide
The honor and privilege to walk by your side.

To have you complete me in thought, deed, and grace
Seeing you love me written all over your face
Knowing you're proud of me for who knows why
Soothing me gently whenever I cry.

You are my windfall, my one happy thought
In all depth of unknowing, it's you that I sought
You are my everything wrapped up in a bow
My physical and spiritual ducks in a row.

The Fortress

Turn your back against the wind
Shade your eyes from the sun
Take the first step on that open trail
Our journey has begun.

Cling always to my tenderness Love
Seek no other council but mine
Create adventures to contain us both
Our lovemaking being the brine.

Show me joy through your eyes Love
Like the hypnotic state of the fire
Offer me what has eluded me thus far
A man's touch, his taste, his desire.

Let me complete you in every way
As enthralling as the hush of the sky
Your beck and call are my second nature
May I seduce you every time that I try.

Your love is now my fortress
The only home I'll ever know
Everything else in this world is absconded
I'll follow you wherever you go.

Your Mercy

I am at your mercy Love
This doesn't instill pride
But one harsh word from your lips
Can whither me inside.

I am your helpless muse Love
To this I do confess
Because I swoon at your feet
Don't think of me any less.

I am a weary traveler
Searching desperately for your love
I would choose you before my dignity
If push came down to shove.

Let me be beside you Love
I've passed life's cruelest test
To be without you for centuries
All while giving the world my best.

Soften the withered corners of me
With the gentleness of your hand
Show me deep compassion
As I help you understand.

Wipe away the dirt-stained tears
That streak across my face
Coax me from the darkest corner
I was told that was my place.

You alone can fix me Love
You're the sanctuary that I depend
Your life blood runs through my veins
With you I can ascend.

Love Realized

I wish you could see you through my eyes
Acknowledge the beauty that you display
Drop all layers of armor
And the impulse to run away.

I wish you would let go Love
Of all your false pretenses
Know all enemies of the past
As friends with their own defenses.

I wish you would stop clinging
To problems and the pains
Let go of all the fear
Nurture then just what remains.

Stop hooking issues into you
With the casual use of 'my'
These are things fed to you by others
Refuse politely to comply.

Wean yourself off compliments
Forgo drama's elusive side
Shift from the mind to heart
Slash empty the sack of pride.

Bash through to your wonderful
Beyond the part called Me
Sear through all the shackles
Allow wonder to gush free

Relax in being untethered
To what has stained your grace
Accept the raw skinned feeling
Truth can sometimes feel like mace.

Gather up the love within
Wrap yourself in its depth
Revel in the victories
The ones conquered when you slept.

See yourself through Love's eyes
Feel you with Love's heart
Know yourself in Love's mind
From love you'll never part.

You are love unencumbered
The full depth of it actualized
Walking you straight into this truth
Makes you Love now realized.

Our Synergy

You are my love
You are my life
I am your muse
I am your wife.

You are my sun
And all far away stars
I am your wire cutter
To all human bars.

You make the sense
To my every reason
I am your windfall
Through every new season.

You supply logic
I bring the play
We make magic happen
Every day.

Steppingstones

All the silly things that we do
Are the steppingstones of our life
From being in sync with each other's ways
To me being your best friend and wife.

I never thought someone as amazing as you
Would be pacing in my future for me
I never knew how fun companionship was
Or how effortless loving can be.

You looked into my soul
You tweezed out each broken chard
Tweezed out each splinter
Pried the gates of our potential free.

You gave me permission to have
What others take for free
Flooded my inner worlds with light
Expanded the boundaries of me.

I never before believed in fate
Except as a cruel joke
But you appeared out of the mist
And removed a heavy yoke.

You play hopscotch on my heart now Love
Chalk out each measured square
However your discernment directs our life
You'll always have me there.

CHAPTER 12

Erotica

I REMEMBER THAT early on in our relationship, Jen would write a love poem for me almost every day. Before long, there was quite the collection of them. And it is funny to recall that Jen did not realize at the time how erotic those poems were. So, she was quite surprised when I suggested that we include them in a chapter of the book entitled Erotica.

While some of the poems are quite suggestive, I think of them as also having a spiritual angle. They reflect the need and desire for human contact and connection. They are also incredibly healing for goddesses all over the world. When thinking about writing this chapter introduction, I asked Jen to lay out the spiritual context of sex and sexuality. Here are her insights on the topic.

People are living breathing portals. Anything that they think, say, or do can be manifested if they start from the heart and propel it into manifestation through their intention. This means heart first, mind second. The problem with this is that people don't realize how empowered they are. They manifest their own limitations when their heart is closed, and the mind is operating on automatic. Most people operate on automatic.

A lot of spiritual people believe that the path to expansion is through meditation. But if meditation becomes a mental exercise, you won't get results you desire and you will begin to think that you are a failure. Without having your heart in it, meditation is an exercise in strengthening the ego. Amplifying the ego moves you farther away from your goal of enlightenment.

One of the most profound ways to touch one's own divinity is through climaxing because of a sexual stimulus. It is a dynamic way of channeling your energy that is usually locked in what is called the kundalini. The kundalini energy is a seemingly omnipotent reserve. But it is not meant to be tapped into by the ego. The way to access it is through the heart center and to pull it up through the root chakra.

But here is the thing. Even the most schooled energy workers still perceive this energy that runs through the chakras with a linear projection. There are pictures depicting energy flowing into the top of the head like a river and down through the chakras. But this is not how it works.

The energy that comes and goes through each chakra is an energy exchange system. Energy is coming in and going out in all directions. This is in perfect synchronicity with the rhythm of all life. Our energy pulses in unison with all of life. But when we limit our understanding of this energy, we bring our mind, body, and emotions out of balance.

Climaxing through love-making is a great way to realign all the energy of the lower bodies – the physical, astral, causal, and mental bodies – with the pulsing greatness of the higher self. When all are aligned, there is wellness and completion in the body.

When two people are making love, the lower bodies are softened through foreplay. The physical body is stimulated, the emotions are raw, the causal body is relaxed, and the mind is liberated from inhibitions and defenses. This is what tantric sex moves are intending to do so that both parties can open to the wonders of higher consciousness together. This is the wonder of climaxing together. It is a spiritual process of touching enlightenment together, if only for a fleeting moment.

The spirituality of lovemaking often gets lost, and it becomes an exercise in the gratification of the lower bodies instead of the wonder that it can be. Female energy has excess emotional energy and male energy is overcompensating in mental energy. When things don't work out so magically in lovemaking, it can be that she is too emotional, and he can't get out of his own head.

Part of the foreplay of lovemaking is to help the other partner give over to you what they have too much of and take from you what you have too much of. Female energy will pour her love and reassurance on her partner. So much so that is allows him to relax the deficiency of his emotional body. In energy it would look like one having an overabundance of energy in one area and sharing it with their partner so that both balance out. They fill each other's deficiencies and take each other's excess.

Male energy will assist his partner by making her feel safe and protected. This allows her to relax the surplus of her emotions and pour her excess into him. This excess makes his energy more receptive to share. Male energy has been trained to take and female energy naturally gives. The spiritual goal in lovemaking is to fill each other up on every level and to allow both parties to both give and receive in the relationship.

When both parties are in total agreement, higher consciousness is met through the climax. Since male energy is trained to take, and female energy is conditioned to give, there is often an imbalance in lovemaking and each party climaxes separately. But the goal is to climax together.

Climaxing together is often difficult to achieve. This is because one or both of the parties do not understand themselves as energy beings and just interact from the point of view of the physical body, emotions, and the mind. This brings frustration in the most loving intentions.

A balanced energy field is like a perfect toroidal field. It is moving flowing energy that is connected to all other beings through their toroidal field. When two bodies come together for love making, the male will ejaculate his energy up through the spine of the woman. Male energy is very direct and female energy is all encompassing. When he shoots his energy through the female body, she adds her climax to his and it creates a dynamic toroidal field bigger than both.

If you do not have a sexual partner, you can practice manifesting toroidal fields through your own climax. There is a sense of completion for many in that experience.

The climax that happens during orgasm has a potential to manifest the most dynamic intentions. This was common knowledge at one point in ancient history. So, to subjugate humans, the sex act was desecrated in several ways to derail individuals from their empowerment.

The focus on making babies is a bait and switch from the real empowerment of women. In Goddess terms, having a baby was the booby prize. The less gifted Goddesses were capable of breeding. The more dynamic Goddesses would not need validation through motherhood. They were respected and even revered for their abilities in working with energy.

Another way to derail the empowerment of love making is through shame. Just as gratitude opens the energy systems of the body, shame closes them. The more shame that is induced on an individual or a sect of people, the more they are removed from their empowerment.

Adopting the SFT tapping protocol is a great way to eliminate the primal programming stored in your DNA regarding sex. It is a way to address the core issues of bias instead of just addressing behavior and symptoms. Eliminating primal programming will enable the collective to transcend.

I trust the practical understanding of the spiritual nature of sex provided by Jen has been illuminating. Without further ado, please enjoy the erotica poems and artwork.

Marvin Schneider
Wodonga, Australia
March 2022

Higher Love

You call to me in the dance of the wind
The sun, the moon, the rain
Each cadence of nature beckons to me
With the same sweet and melodic refrain.

You reach beyond all time and space
Wrap my essence in a silver white song
Whisper in perfect silence to me
Reassure me that I belong.

You riddle my insides with butterflies Love
That only you can command
With a whimsical childlike openness now
I ache to understand.

You mimic the rhythm of my breath
The pound of my heartbeat as well
Your presence is with me everywhere now
It's a blessing my life didn't foretell.

You awaken my body, heart, mind, and soul
To a destiny void of limitation
Freeing the suffering of the whole lower worlds
Is the by-product of our love's manifestation.

Let the whole world now celebrate Love
Through the sanctity of this decree
Together we heal every last soul
Through the process of you loving me.

We offer this upgrade to all atoms of life
On all planets through the celestial sea
May all access the intention of this purest union
As permission to set themselves free.

The Dichotomy

An endless roaring ocean cavern
Leading to a bottomless ravine
A rhythmic rush of thunder
Passing through my worlds unseen.

The quivering of excitement
Tilting on the precipice of fear
Is this all in my imagination?
Do you really want me near?

Trepidation meets the moment
On the steps of hallowed ground
Is this all in my imagination?
Do you even want me around?

Do you agree to dance with me?
Or do I undulate on my own?
Am I myself significant?
Am I enough alone?

You creep into my private chambers
Where no one else can tread
Witness Goddess' evolution
Where vulnerability and empowerment wed.

Oh, what you must think of me
As I struggle in this dichotomy
A lonely love starved desperate waif
Intent on healing all of humanity.

All that You Are

I am your canvas
Paint me as you will
My body is your acreage
Plant your seed and till.

I am your forest
Lay down in my fern
Use me as your tinder
Smolder as I burn.

You are like the wind to me
Calling out my name
An expansive impressionist landscape
Allow me to be your frame.

The moment that I knew of you
Is when my life begun
Now I revel in partaking of you
And to taste me on your tongue.

You are now my windfall
I lay me at your feet
Every moment I breathe you in
You make this world complete.

Please take me with you willingly
Everywhere you go
Experience love through our shared eyes
Share everything that you know.

Dream with me in pristine lands
That exist within the heart
I revel in all that you are
Including when you fart.

Interplay

I am your Goddess
You are my God
We serve all the multitudes
Without worship or laud.

Every love song written
Is dedicated to you
Every birth that is breached
Brings our renewal too.

You flutter my heart strings
With a virtuoso flare
Every pulse is exhilarating
A demonstration that you care.

Our love expounds consciousness
Beyond space, matter, and time
Your power to move through me
Is electric, sublime.

I'll succumb with submission
To your conquistador ways
As we unearth our passions
All our nights and our days.

Guiding Star

You are my captain
I am your sea
Ride me to the ocean
Set all inhibition free.

Pin me up against a break wall
As we ebb and flow
We'll create our own riptide
With a strong undertow.

You are my captain
Take over my helm
I steady your hands on me
So the storm won't overwhelm.

I'll trust your steering
As you move through my cove
Pushing through wild waters
That no other man has dove.

I'll be your compass
Or perpetual guiding star
We'll revel in completion
Wherever we are.

Under the Moon

My love is the ocean
To your calming shore
Eagerly flowing to you
Forever more.

Batten down the hatches
I'll flood every shore
The thirst of the water
Grows for you more.

Man every lighthouse
Send out every ship
Passion is rising
As you touch my lips.

Engulfing your island
As the top of me crests
Falling completely enthralled
On your loving chest.

Drown me in kisses
Flood every lagoon
I'll pleasure you often
Under the moon.

I nibble around your edges
Meet me as I surge
Swim in my waters
As we totally merge.

Battered Goddess

Erase the shame from my body Love
Like only you can do
Lead me through an interplay
That all confident lovers go through.

Pour your seed on my blemishes
Acknowledge every scar
The one place that is sacred for me
Is anywhere you are.

Draw from me the mind fucks Love
That I'll never be enough
Fill that space with your laughter Love
And promises of happier stuff.

Unhinge my habit to recoil
From the cruelty programmed within
Erase from me the admonishments
Reprimands, threats, and sin.

Lead me gently by the hand
To a world of providence
It's an alternate reality to me
Where being loved makes perfect sense.

Gaze upon me always Love
Never with disdain
Erase from me the self-loathing
Where other men have lain.

Expunge the path tore through me Love
Where cruelty left its mark
Till a virgin soil in me
Unabashed, uninhibited, and stark.

Lay your mark upon me Love
Conquer me with your flag
Entertain me with your comical musings
As you overemphasize your swag.

I follow the kindness in your voice
To a kinder reality too
One where I am completely at peace
Simply by being with you.

You alone can heal me love
There's nothing else I can do
The only salvation for this battered Goddess
Is eternity with you.

Calling Your Name

Wrap your arms around me Love
Cup your hand under my breast
Spoon your warmth against me Love
Command me to take rest.

Hold me tenderly in the night
Please never send me away
Reassure me in our lovemaking
Resurrect me with banter and play.

Guide my hand towards your desire
Encourage me to take hold
Delight in confidence you alone provoke
Never chide me for being so bold.

Sink into me often Love
I'll never turn you away
I thrive in the glory and revel of you
As you straddle me where I lay.

Conquer the worlds where duality dwells
Be my lover and friend just the same
I cry out to the heavens in one sacred prayer
Simply by calling your name.

Love's Pursuit

I taste the salty nectar of you
And hold it on my tongue
Grabbing your attention
Is Goddess' innocent fun.

I hold you captive in my hands
My heart, my mind, and throat
You ride the sea of passion in me
You are the buoy to my boat.

I take you to exotic places
That you alone can't find
You are the God to all my worlds
As we leave this one behind.

I send you on an excursion
That bursts forth in your mind
The thrill of you enthralls me
And I follow you in kind.

We fall together between the sheets
And lay together bare
Some would call this decadent
But as Goddess I don't care.

I will be your fiddle
You will be my flute
We play in perfect harmony
In the name of love's pursuit.

Rising Up to Meet You

I open up my petals to you
Beckon you to take me in
Your allure is as undeniable
As the stubble on your chin.

I rise up to meet you
The other half of me
You know all the ways
To set my passion free

I rise up to meet you
Again and again
There's no one else I respond to
In a whole sea of men.

I rise up to meet you
In anticipation and grace
It's like meeting ecstasy
In your beautiful face.

Our bodies splash together
A profound spiritual hue
We meet God in each other
In everything that we do.

We ebb and flow together
Expand as we part
Our love fills the whole universe
You engorge my whole heart.

The ache of intensity
Floods out from your intent
Leaves me breathless and helpless
As I surrender, content.

Lay yourself over me
Rest for a while
Let me wrap myself around you
As we share a smile.

Stark Truth

The summit of my breasts
Enthusiastically stand erect
Instinctively answering an inner call
From your desire I suspect.

We pull off layers of pretense
That protect us from stark truth
Reclaim our naked abandonment
We flaunted in our youth.

Your form and heat cause shivers
As I spread myself to let you in
There's no means to know in our desire
Where you end, and I begin.

I kiss you round and firmly
You glide through me like an open door
The full of your attention
Excites me even more.

Anything you give to me
Is more than I expect
I open my whole presence to you
In reverence and respect.

You press your body into me
Penetrating my inner core
As one soul we climb together
To access heaven's floor.

Spill your love into me now
Expand my presence too
The angels sing out in delight
As I cry in ecstasy with you.

Eternity's Gate

Rip the layers off me Love
Like only you can do
Undress me from this last façade
That only you see through.

Pour your wine upon my breast
Marvel at its stain
Only as you drink me in
Do I get relief from self-disdain.

Lower all your weight on me
Cover me like dew
Relieve me of this burden I wear
By gifting me with you.

Steady all my trembling limbs
Wipe away one last tear
Being in this world without you Love
Is my only fear.

Yet, I can battle heaven and hell
Wrap them in a bow
If it helps you to succeed
If it helps you grow.

You my Love hold all the power
You command my fate
I exist only in the presence of you
As we enter eternity's gate.

Reminder

Gently bend me over
Lay me on the floor
Push your love into me
Have me beg for more.

Splash me with your sweat
Cover me like dew
Collapse into my body
Stick to me like glue.

I'll wear your scent like perfume
You in turn wear mine
To remind us where our love dwells
Between this world and the divine.

Complete Me

Spray your rays all over me
Like sun upon my face
Surprise me with a facial
Cover me with lace.

Command my skin to drink you in
Your soothing natural balm
Play me like your instrument
My breasts erected by your palm.

Tangle me in intrigue
That only lovers know
Tie me to your bedpost
Wrap me in a bow.

Coerce me with your soft tongue
Thrust pleasure in my heart
Absolve me of self-consciousness
As you spread my legs apart.

Bless me with your know-how
Absolve me of all sin
Take the shame I'm wrapped in
And pop it with a pin.

You alone can have me love
In every way you can
You complete me as a woman
Let me complete you as a man.

Healing Goddess

Crush the memories of the others
As you press yourself into me
Purge their stain from my body
Set my inhibitions free.

Soak my skin with your desire
Wash away the shame
Purify my essence with your touch
Pardon me of blame.

Believe me when I declare
There is no one else but you
Feel my passion pulse again
As we do what we are compelled to do.

Let our bodies rise and fall
In synchronicity
Your gentle firm caresses
Are healing salve for me.

Cover me with kisses
To moisten our desire
Mold me to your embrace
To stoke my inner fire.

You alone can sanctify
What others dropped in my path
Sanitize what they defiled
Squelch a Goddess' wrath.

You give back to Goddess
What other men have taken
Pay homage to me in your bedchamber
Let all the world awaken.

Postscript

IT WAS SUCH AN HONOR to write the foreword and chapter introductions to Jen Ward's collection of poems. In this postscript, I will share with you the aspirations that Jen and I have in uplifting all of humanity through The CAUSE Initiative.

My life's purpose is to lead the transformation of the global business and investment communities to create wealth on an ongoing basis in ways that enhance the wellbeing of the individual, the wider community, and the environment. This purpose is underpinned by a noble intent to uplift all of humanity and bring the global business and investment communities into higher consciousness.

CAUSE is an acronym that stands for *Commerce Acting to Uplift Society (Exponentially)*.

It is important that businesses create wealth. But it will become increasingly evident that ongoing wealth creation can only occur when societal wellbeing is enhanced through the activities of the business and investment communities. We are getting to a tipping point where this premise will be widely accepted as a self-evident truth.

Companies that transform themselves in a manner consistent with The CAUSE Initiative principles will deliver excellent operating, financial, capital market and ESG (Environmental, Social and Governance) outcomes.

Institutional investment firms that transform themselves in a manner consistent with The CAUSE Initiative principles will deliver excellent long-term sustainable investment returns on behalf of retirees. They will also foster an environment in which to encourage the transformation of companies through their constructive ownership engagement activities.

Many forward-thinking business leaders around the world are already philosophically aligned with this understanding. Some are already exhibiting the fortitude and courage to transform their organizations to enable them to create wealth on an ongoing basis in ways that enhance societal wellbeing. Others are caught in the mire of the intersection between old and new paradigm consciousness. As a result, they are not yet taking the necessary transformation actions. And sadly, there is still a high proportion of business leaders that are stuck in the old and corrosive business paradigm where the focus in on maximizing short-term profits at all costs.

The unfortunate reality is that most large corporations are heavily vested in old paradigm consciousness, strategies, business models, systems, structures, processes, cultures, and leadership styles. They typically have a significant amount of capital invested in infrastructure that will quickly become worthless and will represent at best a stranded asset, and at worst a liability to the company. They require a significant amount of transformation effort to consciously move the dial closer towards what will inevitably be viewed as 'the gold standard.'

Moving the dial in this way will require leadership, courage, and fortitude. In many cases, it will require Boards and C-suite executives to:

- fundamentally rethink their purpose;
- recognize which aspects of their existing business model are no longer fit for purpose;
- invest to develop new products and services that are truly worthy in the eyes of consumers;
- develop new ways to produce and distribute those products and services to minimize harm and ultimately enhance the wellbeing of the individual, the wider community, and the environment; and
- put in place the internal systems, processes, culture, and leadership capabilities for long-term, ongoing, and sustainable wealth creation.

This is clearly a large scale and multi-year transformation journey. It requires courage, vision, passion, and leadership. It also requires the support and backing of institutional investors.

It is in recognition of this that I have developed The CAUSE Initiative. The CAUSE Initiative will bring together an ecosystem of key participants to consciously encourage, support and drive the transformation of the global business and investment communities for the benefit of all of humanity.

The CAUSE Initiative is centered around a series of activities, including:

- partnering with several leading business schools to be the stewards of, and further develop and distribute the intellectual property that underpins key aspects of The CAUSE Initiative;
- engaging with business leaders and peak bodies of influence from around the world to advocate for the change required for the business and investment communities to be of true service to society;

- partnering with a global strategy consulting firm to roll-out the systematic business transformation consulting services centered on The CAUSE Initiative principles and frameworks;

- partnering with several large institutional investment firms to embed within them an investment and ownership engagement approach centered on The CAUSE Initiative principles and frameworks;

- partnering with several firms that undertake sell-side equities research to significantly enhance, differentiate and reimagine their equities research capabilities centered on The CAUSE Initiative principles and frameworks; and

- partnering with a large-scale financial data services provider to develop a subscription data service targeted at companies and investors, which contains a wide array of unique financial and capital market performance metrics focused on ongoing wealth creation.

It is fairly evident that the business and investment communities currently operate with a high degree of self-interest and indifference as to the impact of their activities on the wider community.

But when you think about it from a higher vantage point, the business and investment communities are just an extension of the wider community. Their employees, suppliers and regulators are also their customers, and are part of the wider community in which companies have a license to operate. Therefore, it makes sense that the business and investment communities should act to enhance societal wellbeing – because in doing so, they are creating the conditions for their own long-term success and legitimacy.

So how did the business and investment communities get it so wrong and skewed over the last five decades or more?

The simple answer may lay in the corrosive intersection between self-interest, indifference, primal consciousness, short-termism, and the intoxicating yet damaging dogma popularized by Milton Friedman and the Chicago school of economics.

That school of thought posited that the primary (and even singular) goal of business is to maximize profit. It is largely indifferent as to how to achieve that objective. But advocates of the theory tend to prioritize aggressive competition, economic efficiency, deregulation, market forces, short-term profit maximization, and shareholders over stakeholders.

Some of these ideas were either written into or assumed to exist within corporations' law. They quickly became the dominant theory underpinning the notion of the fiduciary duty of Directors. Over time, this kind of thinking led to the perverse executive remuneration structures and payouts that we still observe across many large, listed corporations across the Western world.

So entrenched was this kind of thinking, that for many business leaders, any hint or whisper of the notion of a broader corporate purpose beyond maximizing value for shareholders (using short-term profit maximization as a proxy) was akin to promoting a socialist agenda.

So why have business and investment community leaders not been called to account sooner? And when can we expect to see a tipping point when the thinking underpinning The CAUSE Initiative will become mainstream?

The answer to these questions may lay in the notion of human consciousness and the extent to which the broader community becomes more attuned to, and able to access, higher consciousness.

The broader community is increasingly becoming aware of and attuned to the notion of higher consciousness and noble purpose. In their simple forms, practices such as mindfulness, meditation, sound healing, and yoga as pathways to access higher consciousness are becoming mainstream within society.

As this trend continues, there will be a point in time when the broader community will no longer tolerate the kind of behavior and outcomes resulting from old paradigm business consciousness. Business leaders that doggedly cling to old paradigm consciousness and behaviors will be held to account, will be moved aside, and their companies will cease to be relevant. Even those that are firmly entrenched within the shareholder primacy paradigm must be concerned about the inevitable destruction of shareholder value that a failure to act will surely precipitate.

This book, and the spiritual principles explored within each of the chapter introductions, provides the foundation upon which to appreciate the power and necessity of a noble intention for business, higher purpose, operating from a higher vantage point, higher consciousness, and ultimately, being able to easily tap into direct knowingness.

These topics are important in a business context. This is because the key to ongoing wealth creation is noble purpose centric innovation and creativity. Innovation and creativity centered on a noble purpose is most easily institutionalized when many people within the organization can access higher consciousness in a process that is otherwise known as 'tapping into direct knowingness.' That is why it is beneficial to consider these philosophical perspectives and allow them to exist within the business and investment communities. It is about bringing the heart and soul back to business after many decades of the business and investment communities having lost their moral compass.

Many highly creative and intuitive people recognize that their best ideas come fully formed in the mind at the point of disconnecting with an issue that they are passionately interested in. This 'eureka moment' phenomenon; in which there is a moment of sudden, triumphant discovery, inspiration, or insight; is no random occurrence. It is real. It is not the leftfield imagining of new age hippies.

Albert Einstein is often quoted as having said things like 'I didn't arrive at my understanding of the fundamental laws of the universe through my rational mind'; and 'The intellect has little to do on the road to discovery. There comes a leap in consciousness, call it intuition or what you will, where the solution comes to you, and you don't know how or why.' While these quotes often go unreferenced to known source writings, they do express the sentiment being explored here. And they are consistent with the widely attributed Einstein quote, 'The intuitive mind is a sacred gift, and the rational mind is a faithful servant. We have created a society that honors the servant and has forgotten the gift.'

It is certainly my experience that innovation and creativity – the foundations of ongoing wealth creation – are processes that tap into direct knowingness and work within the realms of intuition rather than rational or logical analysis.

Many of the most important and 'over the horizon' aspects of the frameworks, tools and capabilities that underpin The CAUSE Initiative have come to me in this way. My eureka moments often come to me in the REM part of my dream cycle just prior to waking up. This is particularly the case after having actively and passionately engaged on an issue the day before. Then when I am awake, and having shaven, showered, and dressed for the day, I can outflow and create without much effort or thought. In fact, I often find that the outflowing ceases when I lower my vantage point by engaging the rational mind.

I attribute my ability to tap into direct knowingness in this way to my decades long journey in understanding and mastering the spiritual principles described in this book. Central to that journey is the understanding that there is a universal consciousness that all souls are connected to, and when properly attuned to, can be tapped into.

There is a lot of work to be done to transform the global business and investment communities along the lines described here.

A broad cross section of people operating within the business and investment communities need to shift their vantage point to encompass the principles and understandings expressed in this book. Jen has a big role to play in this respect. She works tirelessly in private sessions and other media outlets to help clients release core issues and then see themselves as an aspect of Source having a human experience. This shift in vantage point is so important because without it, business leaders will be unwilling to turn away from greed and self-interest in favor of creating wealth by being of service to society.

My role in the transformation process is more tangible in nature. It involves working with business leaders and other members of The CAUSE Initiative ecosystem to make the specific changes required for businesses and institutional investors to walk the talk. My expectation is that most of the 16,500 very large, listed companies in the world will require a significant amount of 'on the ground' work over a period of three to five years. There is enough work here to keep me fully utilized for the rest of this incarnation.

What is really cool about all of this is the way that Jen and I operate in synergy. The success of my work is contingent on the work that Jen does in uplifting each individual and the broader human collective. At the same time, the collective will find it easier to operate within the less harsh vibration of an environment where business is truly operating as a force for good.

I encourage everyone to support the tireless work that we are doing to uplift all of humanity.

Marvin Schneider
Wodonga, Australia
March 2022

Index

A Distant God, 39
A New Person, 114
A Portal of God, 21
A Series of Blessings, 132
A State of Being, 13
All Life, 22
All that You Are, 304
All This and More, 147
An Easy Sell, 223
Angel's Hue, 208
Any Day, 84
Artistry, 106
Assistance, 188
Awakening, 104
Balance, 17
Battered Goddess, 308
Beautiful Androgyny, 66
Beauty, 255
Being Invisible, 279
Being Present, 18
Being With You, 271

Between the Stillness and the Sky, 145
Bless This Day, 238
Bonded in Purpose, 55
Book of Life, 227
Buying Freedom, 43
Calling Your Name, 310
Celebrating the Moment of Now, 234
Commitment to Me, 183
Complete Me, 317
Discernment, 229
Ducks in a Row, 289
Empowerment, 144
Encouragement, 244
Encouragement of a Full Moon, 121
Enlightenment, 119
Eternity's Gate, 315
Every Angel, 103
Gaia Speaks, 86

Gaining Spiritual Maturity, 134
Getting to the Heart of It, 51
Give a Life Its Due, 53
GMOs, 80
God or Source, 167
Goddesses' Plea, 142
Guiding Light Source, 198
Guiding Star, 306
H$_2$0, 82
Healers Reunite, 179
Healing All Souls, 160
Healing Goddess, 318
Higher Love, 302
Homage to the Foliage, 76
Homage to You, 251
How to Transcend, 120
How?, 143
Human Victory, 23
Humanity, 36
Humanity's Greatest Vice, 189
Humanity's Heart, 278
I Am Love, 38
I Honor You, 162

I'm Me, 131
In Your Eyes, 284
Incarnating, 109
Individuality, 16
Integrity's By-Laws, 239
Integrity's Blueprint, 235
Interplay, 305
Life's Monument, 41
Live Life Boldly!, 256
Living in Zen, 107
Loneliness, 277
Love in the End, 19
Love Is All You Are, 214
Love Realized, 292
Love's Compassion, 219
Love's Pursuit, 311
Loved on All Sides, 252
Love's Appeal, 230
Love's Beautiful Array, 49
Love's Best Lesson, 59
Love's Call, 273
Love's Final Decree, 236
Love's Own Decree, 136
Loving by Default, 182
Mastery, 117
May All Blessings Be, 7

Meet Me Halfway, 185
Men of Goddess, 127
Monastery, 129
More than Family, 83
Mortar and Sticks, 79
My Alchemy, 173
My Altar, 155
Omnicience, 113
One Ancient Celestial Tune, 260
One and the Same, 88
One Little Human The Dichotomy, 249
One Little Human, 248
One Loving Plea, 169
One Thought of You, 282
One Worthy Goal, 165
Our Synergy, 294
Perceiving in Energy, 14
Permission, 187
Proving Me Wrong, 191
Pure Love, 12
Qualities, 166
Reminder, 316
Rising Up to Meet You, 312
Search and Rescue, 269

Second Sight, 34
Self-Realization, 116
Senses, 171
Shadows Come Alive, 35
Sighting, 78
Silent Majority, 57
Sing, 228
Soul Trail Blazer, 108
Speaking for the Unborn, 61
Spiritual Marriage, 168
Stand Still, 275
Stark Truth, 314
Stepping Stones, 295
Surrender, 170
That's What You Do, 110
The Apathy of Man, 10
The Awakened, 105
The Betterment of You, 154
The Celebration, 221
The Defense, 196
The Depth of You, 240
The Dichotomy, 303
The Empath, 130
The Example, 44
The Fight, 9

The Fortress, 290

The Gift of This Life's Struggle, 31

The Golden Thing, 140

The Miracle of You, 253

The Moment, 85

The Replanting, 194

The Rescue, 285

The Sledgehammer, 64

The Tiny Fleet of Sandy Hook Angels, 62

The Troubadour, 262

The Ultimate Goal, 172

The Valley Past Time, 156

The Wayshower, 212

The Winter Rose, 195

The Worthiest Goal, 287

Thrill Ride, 141

Through Your Eyes, 192

To Empower the World, 159

To Finally Expound, 67

Transcendence, 101

True Abundance, 257

True Strength, 258

Truth, 217

Turning Point, 210

Under the Moon, 307

We Can, 232

What It Is to Be Free, 118

What Needs to Happen to Have Peace, 47

What Would Dr. Seuss Say?, 245

What You Are Capable Of, 254

When, 216

When Childhood Goes Wrong, 200

Where Truth and Love Began, 220

Why?, 288

Winning the Human Race, 99

Within You, 218

Wounded Goddess, 181

Yet, 250

You Are the Victor, 164

You Exponentially, 225

Your Average Best Friend, 60

Your Friend, 122

Your Happiness, 158

Your Mercy, 291

ABOUT THE AUTHOR

Jen Ward is a dynamic healer, performance coach and group facilitator. She has devoted her life to helping others unlock their true potential. She is also an accomplished writer and poet.

Jen's extraordinary and challenging personal journey has gifted her with a unique ability to perceive in energy and read akashic records. This, along with her Spiritual Freedom Technique (SFT) taps, allows Jen to work with clients to remove blockages to happiness and effectiveness that exist within any individual.

Jen's goal in publishing this book is to help people connect with their spirituality and transcendence through poetry. A lot of her poems are inspired by talking to the trees outside of her previous home in Rochester, New York.